# God whispers

learning to hear His voice

by Margaret Feinberg

# God Whispers

Published by Relevant Books
A division of Relevant Media Group, Inc.

*www.relevant-books.com*
*www.relevantmediagroup.com*

Design by **Relevant Solutions**
Bobby Jones, Daniel Ariza, Greg Lutze
*www.relevant-solutions.com*

International Standard Book Number: 0-9714576-1-1

For information:
RELEVANT MEDIA GROUP, INC.
POST OFFICE BOX 951127
LAKE MARY, FL 32795
407-333-7152

04 05 9 8 7 6 5 4 3 2

Printed in the United States of America

# CONTENTS

*To my Dad and Mom*

Thank you for so many years of unending love and support. You have lived the Christian life as it was meant to be lived—with reckless abandon to Christ. It's an example and gift I will treasure forever.

You can reach Margaret Feinberg by writing:

Margaret Feinberg

PMB 192 1625 Midvalley Dr. #1

Steamboat Springs, CO 80487

email: mafeinberg@juno.com

# INTRODUCTION

Before you begin the adventure of hearing God's voice, let me ask you a question. Why do you want to hear from God? Really. Put down this book for a moment and think about it. What's your motive? What is it you want to hear? Is there something you're longing to know?

It's a tough question, but one only you can answer. It's one you need to answer. Why? Because before you continue reading, you need to come to terms with a simple principle: *God may never answer your concern in the way or time frame you would like Him to respond.*

Hearing from God requires you to give up your own agenda. You have to hand over the program. You have to come to terms with the fact He may never answer you on certain issues. Yes, He will respond on many, but sometimes He chooses to remain silent. There are specific things He may choose not to tell you for years.

Are you willing to wait? Are you willing to be patient? Are you willing to trust Him?

Because learning to hear from God isn't as much about obtaining information as it is about the One who informs. It's not as much about what is said as it is about the One who says it.

As humans, we are naturally more concerned with the destination than the journey. Like young children on a long road trip, we want to know: *Where we are going? When will we get there? What is it going to be like?* In a flurry of questions we become so focused on one issue—what's next—that we fail to enjoy, embrace, and appreciate the moment, the view, and the one who is driving the car.

So the question you need to answer before you go any further is simply: Are you waiting to hear from God on a particular issue? If so, what is it? Maybe it's a job. Maybe it's the person you're going to marry. Maybe it's when or if God will grant you a child. Maybe it's when you are going to fulfill a lifelong calling or dream.

Those are all legitimate issues. God knows them. Are you willing to turn them over to Him? Are you willing to trust God? Are you willing to give up listening for what you want to hear and begin listening to what He wants to speak?

You may want to talk about your occupation, but He may want to raise the issue of your attitude. You may want to discuss your future, but He may want to strengthen your faith. You may want to get out of a situation God has specifically placed you in. You may be asking Him a certain "why" question, and He just wants you to trust Him.

To hear from God, you need to learn to come to Him on His terms, not your own. Recognizing God's voice isn't as much about the voice as it is about God deepening your relationship with Him.

Learning to hear from God isn't always easy. You can't just hook up a phone line or request a memo. There aren't any shortcuts or six-step programs. There is no guarantee you won't collect a few bumps and bruises along the way. Like other spiritual disciplines, it is something you will have to develop and cultivate. It takes time, but its rewards are eternal.

This is a basic, practical guide on how to hear God's voice. It begins by exploring the human hunger to hear from God and His desire to speak. It explains the importance of hearing God's voice and some of the common ways He communicates. It addresses questions and issues that naturally arise as you begin to recognize God's whispers. It ends with challenging you in your relationship with Him.

The chapters are salted with testimonies from dozens of everyday people who have heard from God. Their stories are as diverse as the people themselves. Read them. Study them. You might be surprised to find one or two that echo your own experience with God.

This book doesn't contain all or even most of the answers related to this enormous topic. It is just a launching pad. It gives you some suggestions, offers recommendations, and points you in the right direction. Learning to hear from God isn't a destination as much as it is a big journey, and if you travel far enough you will find yourself abiding in the very heart of your Creator.

It is my hope and prayer that God whispers will become a normal part of your spiritual journey, and He will become the highlight of your every day.

—*Margaret Feinberg*

"A spiritual kingdom lies all about us, enclosing us, embracing us, altogether within reach of our inner selves, waiting for us to recognize it."

—A.W. Tozer[1]

*when hungry hearts meet*

Nearly 1,800 miles of water had passed since they began their journey on their newly purchased boat. Marjane and Bill were destined to the out islands of the Caribbean as missionaries, but along the way they experienced a long list of setbacks. A water pump broke. The refrigeration went out. The weather was too hot in some places and too cold in others. Several cold fronts slowed their journey.

They were nearing their final destination in South Florida before heading out to sea. Marjane knew it wasn't going to be an easy passage. They had to pass through a narrow, rocky inlet known for its strong tides and large waves. Intimidated by the prospect, Marjane said a quiet prayer and went to sleep.

When she awoke, it was strangely quiet. She popped her head above deck only to discover a calm wind, the brightly shining sun and glassy sea. Their vessel, the Maranatha, passed through the unusually peaceful inlet without hindrance. Marjane offered another quiet prayer in thanks to God for the beautiful day. Nearing the end of a long, exhausting journey, she could sense God smiling down on them.

Outside the inlet, Marjane noticed a skywriting plane overhead. She could hear the roaring engine and carefully watched its maneuvers expecting to read an ad for a happy hour or swimsuit sale from one of the local businesses trying to attract tourists. Instead, the plane scripted a perfectly round smiley face in the sky. Marjane laughed aloud, "God, you really are smiling down on us!"

Then, she watched the plane carefully script the words, "God loves you." Before flying away, the pilot added a puffy exclamation point.

Marjane is the first to admit that in her more than thirty years as a Christian, this was the first and only time God used a skywriting plane to speak to her. "I kept thinking, 'God, You're too much,'" she recalls. "It seemed too plain, too direct, too easy. Yet, the message was so clear." Eight hours later, after an enjoyable passage, they arrived at their final destination.

To some, the story seems far-fetched, but to those who line the pages of the Bible, the story seems almost, well, normal. With so many accounts of wild phenomena (burning bushes, talking donkeys, bright stars), skywriting planes seem almost ordinary.

Deep down inside, most Christians really want to hear from God. We would welcome anything that makes life's journey easier, the right decisions clearer, and the future a little bit more predictable, even if it involves a noisy skywriting plane. We want to know we are on the right track, we are headed in the right direction, and everything is going to turn out okay. We want to know God has not forgotten about us. He really does love us. And He really is involved in our lives.

That's one reason why those moments He communicates—God whispers—are so important. They steady our feet when the footing of life seems unstable. They shine a light when the path grows dim. They remind us we are not alone when there is not another soul around who understands.

God whispers are a much-needed part of life. Scripture is laced with them. When God formed the world, He created it with His voice. Behind all the wonders in nature is His spoken word. His voice.

With the simple echo, "Let there be light," brightness filled the expanse. God did not waste any time. He quickly dubbed the light "day" and darkness "night." He called forth an "expanse in the midst of the waters," and the heavens were formed. A request for the "waters below the heavens (to) be gathered into one place" resulted in dry land (Genesis 1).

From the first moments in the Garden of Eden, mankind was introduced to the voice. Adam and Eve communed with their Creator. When they called out to God, they didn't get silence. They heard His voice. They knew Him. They saw His nature reflected in nature. They recognized Him within His design. They enjoyed His company. They waited with great anticipation for His presence; His visits were the highlight of their day.

When the Lord spoke to Adam in the Garden, He didn't have to identify Himself. Adam didn't wonder if he was imagining a voice in his head. He didn't debate the source of the voice. Why? Because Adam knew the One who was speaking.

Genesis doesn't reveal how long the time in the Garden lasted. It quickly transitions to explain how one act of disobedience broke the glass of perfect communion. Take a look at Genesis 3:8-13:

> Then the man and his wife heard the sound of the LORD God as he was walking in the garden in the cool of the day, and they hid from the LORD God among the trees of the garden. But the LORD God called to the man, "Where are you?"

> He answered, "I heard you in the garden, and I was afraid because I was naked; so I hid."

And he said, "Who told you that you were naked? Have you eaten from the tree I commanded you not to eat from?"

The man said, "The woman you put here with me—she gave me some fruit from the tree, and I ate it."

Then the LORD God said to the woman, "What is this you have done?"

The woman said, "The serpent deceived me, and I ate."

If you take time to reflect on Genesis 2 and 3, you will discover God did not stop communicating with mankind after the fall. He didn't lose His voice with the original sin. In fact, the first record of God dialoguing with man is *after* the fruit was eaten.

The Lord pronounced curses on Adam, Eve, and the serpent, but nowhere in the text is there any mention of God limiting mankind's ability to hear from Him. Man may limit his own ability to commune with God—through free will and sin—but God never limits His ability to commune with man.

Following Adam and Eve's dismissal from the Garden, an angel was stationed to keep mankind out of Eden, but nothing could keep God in the Garden. He continued to love and pursue mankind.

Adam and Eve lost access to the Garden, but they never lost God. When the original couple stepped across Eden's boundary, they didn't travel alone. God went with them, and He continued to speak to them. He longed to speak to them, just like He is longing to speak to you.

Do you realize whatever desire you have to hear God pales in comparison to God's desire to speak to you? He hungers to speak to you. He hungers to listen to you. He hungers to commune with you. He hungers for you.

The hunger for communion did not end in the Gard
began there. The Scripture is threaded with individu;
municated with God.

God didn't just speak to Adam and Eve. He went on to speak to
their children and their children's children and their children's
children's children and so on through the ages. Scripture reveals
that God spoke to Cain (Genesis 4:6-7), Noah (Genesis 6:13-21),
Abram (Genesis 12:1-3), and Hagar (Genesis 21:17).

First Samuel 3:4 records the Lord calling to Samuel as a young
boy, to which he finally responded, "Here I am" (NAS). The
simple answer launched Samuel into a remarkable journey of
serving and obeying God.

Consider Hebrews 11, often referred to as the "Hall of Faith"
chapter of the Bible. The vast majority of those listed clearly heard
from God, their specific stories recorded in the Old Testament.
Abraham. Isaac. Jacob. Moses. From the opening declaration, "Let
there be light," in Genesis 1:3 to the final reminder, "Yes, I am
coming soon," in Revelation 22:20, God's voice echoes
throughout Scripture.

Not only did He speak to His people and through His people, He
even appeared to them. He appeared to Abram in Genesis 12:7,
Isaac in Genesis 26:2-5 (and again in Genesis 26:24), and
Solomon in 1 Kings 3:5 and 1 Kings 9:2. His voice and presence
thundered in the heavens throughout the Old Testament, and
God sent His only Son to convey His Word in flesh in the New
Testament.

There are some scholars who would contend God quit speaking
after Christ was born or resurrected, but none of those assertions
are biblical. There are portions in the Gospels and throughout the
New Testament when God spoke directly to His people.

God's voice echoed in the heavens when Jesus emerged from His baptism in the Jordan. With river water still streaming down his face, an audible voice declared, "This is My beloved Son, in whom I am well-pleased."

God spoke during the transfiguration. Peter, James and John were taken up a high mountain where they watched Jesus transform before them. It was there "His clothes became dazzling white, whiter than anyone in the world could bleach them" (Mark 9:3).

During that dramatic scene, Elijah and Moses appeared and began talking with Christ. Mark 9:7 records, "Then a cloud appeared and enveloped them, and a voice came from the cloud: 'This is my Son, whom I love. Listen to him!'"

Even after Christ was crucified and resurrected, God continued to speak publicly and even audibly to mankind. Saul and those around him heard God speak audibly on the road to Damascus. In the Acts 9:3-7 story, a light from heaven flashed around Saul, and he fell to the ground. He heard a voice ask him, "Saul, Saul, why do you persecute me?" To which he responded, "Who are you, Lord?" According to the account, the men traveling with Saul were speechless; they heard the sound but did not see anyone.

On the island of Patmos, John heard a voice behind him that resembled "the sound of a trumpet" (Revelation 1:10) commanding him to write the book of Revelation and send it to seven churches. In the specific messages to those churches listed in Revelation 2 and 3, John adds a consistent message: "He who has an ear, let him hear what the Spirit says to the churches."

God is not bound by a moment in time—whether in the Garden, at the birth of Christ or after His resurrection—to speak to His people. As believers, it is our responsibility to listen.

In Deuteronomy 6:3, God commanded Moses with the opening words, "Hear, O Israel." The same command followed in Deuteronomy 6:4, 9:1, 20:3 and 33:7. In Isaiah 51:7, God invites,

"Hear me, you who know what is right, you people who have my law in your hearts."

God is speaking to His people, but far too many people are missing, or misunderstanding, Him. This is illustrated in John 12:23-28:

> Jesus replied, "The hour has come for the Son of Man to be glorified. I tell you the truth, unless a kernel of wheat falls to the ground and dies, it remains only a single seed. But if it dies, it produces many seeds. The man who loves his life will lose it, while the man who hates his life in this world will keep it for eternal life. Whoever serves me must follow me; and where I am, my servant also will be. My Father will honor the one who serves me.

> "Now my heart is troubled, and what shall I say? 'Father, save me from this hour'? No, it was for this very reason I came to this hour. Father, glorify your name!"

> Then a voice came from heaven, "I have glorified it, and will glorify it again."

This is an amazing passage. In a difficult moment for Christ, one in which He even conceded His heart was troubled, He continued to seek His Father's glory. Then, in a sudden outburst, God not only answered Christ but those around with the promise of present and future glory.

The unusual part about this passage isn't Christ's transparency or God's bold response, but rather how the people who witnessed this event reacted. Verse 29 records, "The crowd that was there and heard it said it had thundered; others said an angel had spoken to him."

God spoke, but some of the crowd heard a storm brewing while others mistook the voice as some sort of angelic visitation. Those who heard the thunder didn't hear the message, and those who believed an angel had spoken didn't recognize the true Messenger. They heard a noise, they just didn't know who it was from or what it said. A closer look at the passage reveals that the crowds—the majority of people listening to God and following Jesus—didn't recognize God's voice. How often do we miss recognizing God when He is speaking to us?

Despite all the misunderstanding, Jesus says, "This voice was for your benefit, not mine" (v. 30). Even though the people didn't fully understand, God spoke for their benefit, and God continues to speak for our benefit.

Why is it so important to listen? Because God is a communicator. He is constantly trying to raise our awareness of Him. And His messages are precious. His words are important. His insights are valuable.

## A MUCH NEEDED VOICE

Now, more than ever, we live in a world where we need to hear God's voice. There are so many voices vying for our attention. While the divas duke it out on daytime television, the liberals and conservatives try to convince us of their political views. Brands fight to get our loyalty. Advertisers spend billions trying to gain our favor. Stores compete to get our visits. Banks battle to get our accounts. And the credit card companies, well, they can't help but mail low introductory offers every few days. We live in a world where everyone wants a part of us. But what we really need is to hear from God.

Hearing the voice may be more important than you realized. Here's why: *You make decisions based on what you hear and know.* If you are not hearing from God—whether through His Word or through spending time with Him—then what will you base your decisions on? Who will win the war for your attention? Your decisions? Your heart?

Whether it's a person you want to marry, a move you want to make, or a job you want to take, you would like to know what God thinks. But God doesn't just want to speak in regard to the "big" decisions in life (and you don't want to have to test out your listening skills on those "big" ones either).

The fact is, God wants to speak into all aspects of your life. He wants to be big in the little stuff. He wants to invade your life—all of it—not just those areas where you think you need Him. He is not interested in having a part of you; He wants all of you.

God wants to speak into areas of your life you have never even considered. He wants to give you words and wisdom you didn't think were possible. He desires to do exceedingly more than you can hope or expect. First Corinthians 2:9 promises: "No eye has seen, no ear has heard, no mind has conceived what God has prepared for those who love Him."

That truth is, you need God in your decision making process. He knows how to help you avoid the pitfalls and not get lost along the journey of life.

*It is God's will that you hear and obey His voice.* In John 10:27-28, Jesus declared, "My sheep listen to my voice; I know them, and they follow me. I give them eternal life, and they shall never perish; no one can snatch them out of my hand."

Jesus spoke of a living relationship with us. Not only does He know us, but we are to know Him and follow Him. Just as a shepherd leads sheep with His voice, so it is Christ's intention to lead us with His voice. Proverbs 15:31 says, "He whose ear listens to the life-giving reproof will dwell among the wise" (NAS). God doesn't just want us to know about Him; God wants us to know Him intimately. He desires for us to recognize His voice.

*God has specific plans for your life you need to hear.* Jeremiah 29:11 says, "'For I know the plans I have for you,' declares the LORD, 'plans to prosper you and not to harm you, plans to give you hope and a future.'"

To bring about His plans, the Lord often has to lead and direct you. It is important to continually hear from the Lord, because He usually does not reveal the entire plan at one time. He may tell you to start a Bible study, but He still wants you to seek Him as to who should attend the study, what it should focus on, and where it should be held.

God also reserves the right to change the game plan. He can change course halfway through a project, surprise you with a new element, or grab your attention through a sudden event. When God moves, move with Him. Be open to Him.

Isaiah 30:21 says, "Whether you turn to the right or to the left, your ears will hear a voice behind you, saying, 'This is the way, walk in it.'" God wants us to depend on the little "rights" and "lefts" that He speaks, and more importantly, to depend on Him.

Elijah discovered this principle early in his ministry as a prophet. In 1 Kings 17 and 18, he is directed and redirected by the Lord three times. First, he is sent to a ravine east of Jordan where he drinks from the brook and ravens feed him. Eventually, the brook dries up, and the Lord sends Elijah to live with a widow at Zarephath. Scripture records "after a long time" he was sent to the evil king Ahab where he eventually defeated the followers of Baal in a fiery showdown.

Now what would have happened if Elijah had never made it past the brook? What if he had followed the first set of instructions and "camped" there, not moving on to the next instructions the Lord gave Him? Would he still have been mightily used of God?

Elijah recognized following God was a journey. He did not camp at the trailhead; he followed the path and kept moving as it twisted and turned until God brought him to his destination, glorifying Him. Just as God had plans for Elijah's life, He has plans for you.

*God's words are valuable.* Bob Hope is one man who knows the value of the written and spoken word. It is something he treasures. Few people know Hope actually has a walk-in vault located in an office compound on his estate. Unlike other vaults, Hope's does not contain any costly antiques, rare paintings, or precious metals. His vault is full of large file drawers. The files contain original pages of jokes submitted by Hope's writers dating back to 1934. They are referenced and cross-referenced with hundreds of topics and subtopics; a check or number in the margin reveals where each joke was used. The collection is worth a fortune.[2]

As Christians, we have the opportunity to develop our own spiritual vaults with lasting treasures—the words of the King. Words that breathe life. Words that bring hope. Words that refresh, challenge, and transform. We are given the opportunity to record them in journals, use them in life lessons, and lock them deep within our hearts where the pages won't tear or soil. We can become rich in our knowledge of Him by studying His Word and spending time with Him.

Did you realize God longs for you to recognize the value of His voice and listen to Him? The longing of God's heart is expressed in Psalm 81:11-13: "But My people did not listen to My voice; and Israel did not obey Me. So I gave them over to the stubbornness of their heart, to walk in their own devices. *Oh that My people would listen to Me, that Israel would walk in My ways!*" (NAS, emphasis added).

Scripture has always placed a premium on hearing God's voice. Deuteronomy 29:29 says, "The secret things belong to the LORD our God, but the things revealed belong to us and to our children forever, that we may follow all the words of this law." God wants to love on us and consume us with His splendor. He wants to do amazing things both in us and through us.

*God will often ask you to do something you would not naturally come up with on your own.* God's plans for your life are much bigger than your own, and He knows what needs to be done in you to bring you to the point where you can be fully used by Him.

Maybe you don't enjoy praying, but God is calling you to a deeper prayer life. Maybe you feel comfortable living in the South, and God is calling to you to take a job in the North. Maybe there are a few people at work you don't really like, but God is calling you to befriend and minister to them.

When you open your heart to God in obedience, He begins to open your eyes to things you've never seen before. He issues frequent invitations for you to become a part of what He is doing.

*Hearing from God heightens your awareness of Him.* Take a moment and picture yourself in a dark room. You are told someone is in the room with you. You wonder about the person's location. How close is the person to you? What is the person doing? It is perfectly quiet. In the silence, you begin to wonder. Then, you begin to doubt. Is there someone else, or are you really alone? You need reassurance.

Out of the darkness, a voice calls out one word—your name. In that instance you know you are not alone; the person is near you. Time passes, and you begin to wonder again. Is the person still in the room? You need a response. Again, the voice echoes a word of reassurance. Now you are confident of one thing: You are not alone.

God's voice reminds you He is with you. It refreshes your faith. It strengthens you. It challenges you. It reassures you that even in the darkest times of life, God is not just watching—He is involved. He will never leave you nor forsake you.

God's voice—His Word—becomes like manna to the Israelites in the desert. It must be sought daily and is necessary for life.

*Hearing from God develops faith.* Hearing from God is birthed through a willing heart, open eyes, and a simple belief God really is speaking to you. You must begin to believe He really is active, engaged, and involved in your life. At the same time, you need to dismiss any notions He is somehow distant or quiet.

In *The Pursuit of God*, A.W. Tozer writes:

> At the root of the Christian life lies belief in the invisible. The object of the Christians' faith is unseen reality. Our uncorrected thinking, influenced by the blindness of our natural hearts and the intrusive ubiquity of visible things, tends to draw a contrast between the spiritual and the real— but actually no such contrast exists. The antithesis lies elsewhere, between the real and the imaginary, between the spiritual and the material, between the temporal and the eternal; but between the spiritual and the real, never. The spiritual is real.
>
> If we would rise into that region of light and power plainly beckoning us through the Scriptures of truth, we must break the evil habit of ignoring the spiritual. We must shift our interest from the seen to the unseen. For the great unseen Reality is God. "He that cometh to God must believe that he is, and that he is a rewarder of them that diligently seek him" (Hebrews 11:6). This is basic in the life of faith. From there we can rise to unlimited heights. "Ye believe in God," said our Lord Jesus Christ, "believe also in me" (John 14:1). Without the first there can be no second. [3]

Faith is developed through the words God speaks. Romans 10:17 says, "Faith comes from hearing the message, and the message is heard through the word of Christ."

As you seek to know God, His will and His involvement in your life, He will reward you with the greatest treasure of all: Himself. Behind every whisper and tucked into every word is an invitation to partake in the Kingdom of God and know the One who sits upon the throne. Your faith, which is more precious than gold, can't help but be strengthened.

*Sometimes the only thing that will give you the courage to keep going is His voice.* You are not a child of circumstance. You are a child of God. Being a child of God means living, speaking, and acting differently. It means giving with whole-hearted abandon, stepping out on faith, and blanketing everything with love. Sometimes being a child of God requires you to stand up against injustice and speak out against sin. It isn't always easy.

Inevitably you will be tempted to compromise. You will be asked to give up, sit down, or take a step back. You will feel pressured to become like everyone else and back down from your God-given convictions.

At those moments a whisper from the Father can make all the difference. It was a whisper that gave Abraham's wife, Sarah, a hope she would have a child when all hope was lost. It was a whisper about building a boat that saved Noah and his family. It was a whisper of promise that strengthened Joseph's faith even when he found himself wrongly imprisoned. A word from God in the right circumstances is "like apples of gold in settings of silver" (Proverbs 25:11).

I stumbled upon this truth in a rather odd and often overlooked passage in the Old Testament. It's found in 1 Samuel 18:19-33 and details one of many difficult moments in the life of David. Absalom, David's son, organized a revolt against his father's authority and usurped his throne forcing David to flee Jerusalem.

Following the uprising, Absalom was killed and a messenger was called to deliver the news to David:

> Now Ahimaaz son of Zadok said, "Let me run and take the news to the king that the LORD has delivered him from the

hand of his enemies."

"You are not the one to take the news today," Joab told him. "You may take the news another time, but you must not do so today, because the king's son is dead."

Then Joab said to a Cushite, "Go, tell the king what you have seen." The Cushite bowed down before Joab and ran off.

Ahimaaz son of Zadok again said to Joab, "Come what may, please let me run behind the Cushite."

But Joab replied, "My son, why do you want to go? You don't have any news that will bring you a reward."

He said, "Come what may, I want to run."

So Joab said, "Run!" Then Ahimaaz ran by way of the plain and outran the Cushite (1 Samuel 19-23).

A watchman standing on the wall reported to David that two messengers were running toward them.

Then Ahimaaz called out to the king, "All is well!" He bowed down before the king with his face to the ground and said, "Praise be to the LORD your God! He has delivered up the men who lifted their hands against my lord the king."

The king asked, "Is the young man Absalom safe?"

Ahimaaz answered, "I saw great confusion just as Joab was about to send the king's servant and me, your servant, but I don't know what it was."

The king said, "Stand aside and wait here." So he stepped aside and stood there.

Then the Cushite arrived and said, "My lord the king, hear the good news! The LORD has delivered you today from all who rose up against you."

The king asked the Cushite, "Is the young man Absalom safe?"

The Cushite replied, "May the enemies of my lord the king and all who rise up to harm you be like that young man."

The king was shaken. He went up to the room over the gateway and wept. As he went, he said: "O my son Absalom! My son, my son Absalom! If only I had died instead of you—O Absalom, my son, my son!" (2 Samuel 18:33)

At first glance, the passage seems like side note. After all, David has just lost his son and regained the throne of Israel. But the author of 2 Samuel takes more than a dozen verses to talk about these two runners who deliver a message to the king.

This entire story puzzled me. What was the point? Why was this included in the Bible? It seemed like an unnecessary addition to the book of 2 Samuel. As much as I wanted to continue reading, I couldn't get past the story. I read it again. Then, I asked the Lord what it meant.

In the still quiet of my spirit, I heard the Lord whisper, "Read it again." I did. Then I questioned the meaning again. His response was the same, "Read it again." I did, and the interchange with the Lord repeated itself until I had read the story more than a half dozen times. It was no use. I decided to give up and go to bed.

The next evening I read the same verses repeatedly, but didn't see anything differently. The third night, I opened my Bible to the now well-worn page and began reading. The story slowly came alive to me.

Ahimaaz, the son of Zadok, was a well-known messenger. In 2 Samuel 17:20, he carried the message from his own father to David telling him to flee across the Jordan. The skilled runner played a key role in protecting the king.

Ahimaaz was fast and knew the local terrain. More than anything, Ahimaaz wanted to deliver the good news to the king. But that's all Ahimaaz wanted to deliver: good news. He wasn't asked to run, and he was even warned there would be no reward, but for his own self-glorification he pleaded to run.

Though he left last, he chose to run the "way of the plain" and arrived in the king's presence first. When the king asked him about Absalom, Ahimaaz lied and said he did not know. David response was slightly chilling: "Stand aside and wait here."

About that time the Cushite arrive. He was a no name guy—literally—his name was never mentioned in the passage. He had chosen the slower, harder route to get to the king and now he was kicking himself for it. For the last leg of the run, all he could see was Ahimaaz's backside—a humiliating reminder that the Cushite's message was old news in the sight of the king.

"Why keep running?" the Cushite probably wondered. "I have been called and chosen to run with this message," he quietly reminded himself.

He approached King David exhausted, gasping for air. He took in a large breath and boldly declared, "My lord the king, hear the good news! The LORD has delivered you today from all who rose up against you."

Then David asked the Cushite the formidable question: "Is the young man Absalom safe?" To which the Cushite delivered the harsh news: The king's son was dead.

It was not a pretty moment in history or the life of David, yet through it the Lord revealed the importance of hearing from Him and being obedient to His whispers. God notices people with great skill, speed, and talent, like Ahimaaz, and He often uses them. But God also has an eye for the no names who aren't the fastest or most talented but who are faithful and have a heart given to obedience.

Being on the slower, less talented side of the fence, I knew God was speaking to me. Like the Cushite, I often see others passing me by in accomplishment and service, but God doesn't want me to be distracted by them. He wants me to be focused on Him and faithful to the calling He's given me.

Maybe you've felt like you've been passed up, too. Maybe you feel like others have gotten to where you're called to be first, and there's no reason for you to keep running. The heartbeat of this passage is an encouragement: keep running. Whatever God has called and chosen for you to do, He will reward you as long as you remain faithful and obedient.

*Hearing God's voice allows you to experience His best for your life.* As humans, we don't have the faintest idea what is best for our lives. We have limited vision. Limited knowledge. Limited everything. Fortunately, there is a limitless God who has an incredible plan for every person's life.

He formed you. He knows you. He knows how you think, act, and respond. He knows how to put you in a place where you will flourish, and He knows how to trim the branches at the right time so you will grow more fruit. He knows what is best for you.

Hearing and obeying God's voice allows you to follow His plan for your life rather than your own. His voice will protect, guide, comfort, and impart life to you. It will allow you to experience the fullness of His blessings.

Undoubtedly, hearing from God will turn your life into a richer adventure. No matter what form He uses—whether Scripture or skywriting—the best part about hearing from God is that it will develop a closer relationship between you and the Father. Are you ready to respond to His voice?

"My sheep listen to my voice; I know them, and they follow me. I give them eternal life, and they shall never perish; no one can snatch them out of my hand."

—John 10:27-30

# why he whispers

God is big. He could use anything to communicate with His people. Think about it. He could fill the sky with a Star Wars presentation, leaving messages beaming in the atmosphere for hours. He could paint His words in nature using everything from tree bark to blooming flowers to freshly fallen snow. He could even use smoke signals or drop parchment from the sky. In modern times, He could send an email, call someone's cell, or leave a voice mail message.

But He doesn't.

He takes a much more subtle approach.

Instead of shouting, He whispers.

Why? Because God is not as interested in imparting information as He is in a relationship. Need proof? Consider the Scripture. If God was in love with data, He would have offered a scientific dissertation on light rather than just uttering the four famed words, "Let there be light," and creating it. The Ten Commandments would be at least ten volumes in length and Jesus' Sermon on the Mount would have put everyone to sleep.

Instead, God is short-winded. And when God speaks, whether through Moses or Christ, everyone who loves Him listens.

One of the main reasons God whispers is to draw you to Him. He is in the business of loving you, maturing you, and conforming you to the image of His Son. He longs to be with you. And along the way, He will drop clues and tidbits about Himself so you can know Him more intimately.

Those waiting for a burning bush experience will probably be disappointed, while those who learn to walk with God and respond to Him—even when it seems like small stuff—will be richly rewarded in their relationship with Him.

Jim Cymbala, pastor of the highly successful and famed Brooklyn Tabernacle in New York City, records one of those God whispering moments on Easter Sunday in 1992. At the end of the evening's service, Cymbala sat down at the edge of the platform exhausted. He was ready to relax and unwind when a homeless man with matted hair and ragged clothing approached him.

Cymbala noticed the man was missing two front teeth, but it was the odor his senses could not escape. The mixture of alcohol, sweat, urine, and garbage took his breath away. In *Fresh Wind, Fresh Fire*, he records:

> I have been around many street people, but this was the strongest stench I have ever encountered. I instinctively had to turn my head sideways to inhale, then look back in his direction while breathing out.
>
> I asked his name.
>
> "David," he said softly.
>
> "How long have you been homeless, David?"
>
> "Six years."
>
> "Where did you sleep last night?"

"In an abandoned truck."

I had heard enough and wanted to get this over quickly. I reached for the money clip in my back pocket.

At that moment David put his finger in front of my face and said, "No, you don't understand—I don't want your money. I'm going to die out there. I want the Jesus that red-haired girl talked about."

I hesitated, then closed my eyes. God, forgive me, I begged. I felt soiled and cheap. Me, a minister of the gospel ... I had wanted simply to get rid of him, when he was crying out for the help of Christ I had just preached about ... He moved toward me and fell on my chest, burying his grimy head against my white shirt and tie. Holding him close, I talked to him about Jesus' love. These weren't just words; I felt them ... And that smell ... I don't know how to explain it. It had almost made me sick, but now it became the most beautiful fragrance to me. I reveled in what had been repulsive just a moment ago.

The Lord seemed to say to me in that instant, *Jim, if you and your wife have any value to me, if you have any purpose in my work—it has to do with this odor. This is the smell of the world I died for.* [4]

On one Easter evening, God whispered a simple but powerful word to an exhausted pastor. It is a word that has followed Cymbala, a man who has seen his church grow from twenty members to more than 6,000 through the years. It is one he holds close to his heart.

But the message from God transcends the situation in which it was delivered. God's words continue to grip countless hearts every time the story is told. Why? Because the message reveals something about God's character. His make-up. His desires. And those who want to know God will naturally want to know what pleases Him.

Whenever God whispers to you—whether it is a word of conviction, revelation, or intercession—He is ultimately trying to draw you closer to Himself. While the initial words may seem overwhelming, unclear, or even strange at first, if they are truly from Him then you will find yourself drawn back to the heart of God.

God's willingness to communicate reflects His heart toward His people. He enjoys His children. He likes being with them, nurturing them, and developing a relationship with them.

Picture a father who comes home from work. He makes a beeline from the front door to his favorite chair and turns on the television. Remote in hand, he flips through the channels until he finds his favorite news anchor. His wife delivers him dinner in his chair, and he remains there until it is time for bed. His children sit silently on the sidelines.

In this scenario, there is no communication between the father and the children. What does it reveal about the father? He isn't overly concerned with his relationship with his children. Compare this scene to the involvement of God since the beginning of time. Someone who walked in the Garden in the cool of the day. Someone who spoke through a burning bush. Someone who sent His only Son to redeem mankind. God does not own a La-Z-Boy. He is active, engaged, and involved. He pursues His children.

Even as a child, God began whispering in my heart. When I was eight years old, the Lord began speaking to me through dreams. I remember being taught in Sunday school that the name of Jesus had power and authority. "So if I say the name of Jesus bad things have to go away?" I asked my mom. "Yes," she replied. "There is power in His name."

That night I went to sleep and dreamed I was cornered on the edge of a steep, rugged cliff by a pack of wolves. I could see their sharp teeth through their ravenous growling and barking. I knew if I didn't do something quickly, I was going to die. I cried out, "In the name of Jesus, go away."

With those words, I watched an invisible sweeping motion shove the wolves over the side of the cliff. I was safe. I woke up vividly remembering the scene. It was a simple dream, but from it I have never doubted the profound power found in the name of Jesus.

A few months later, I had another dream in which I saw a large golden city surrounded by a beautiful gate. It glimmered in the bright light. A city this beautiful must be heaven, I thought to myself. The architecture of the buildings was so unusual. There were large and small structures, but the most noticeable rose above the others with roofs that were round and pointed at the very top.

I thought it strange but creative of God to include Russian-influenced architecture in heaven. I woke up with the rich images in my mind. It wasn't until years later when I saw a photo of Israel's capital in the setting sun that I recognized the city was Jerusalem, not heaven.

In one of the most memorable dreams, though, I was standing at attention in a small army of people. We were lined up perfectly; each of us held a long slender pole in our left hand with a sharpened, crescent moon shaped metal piece at the top. On the platform before us, a few leaders were positioned. One of them was speaking.

Even though I had this dream more than twenty years ago, I still remember his words: "You are here and hold those poles because you have proven yourself worthy. You have been faithful and served the one and true God. You have not fallen away." He went on for some time encouraging us in our devotion to the Lord. Then, he paused and said, "But whoever continues to hold this pole will have their head cut off."

Suddenly the crowd dispersed in mayhem. Many dropped their poles. The men and women around me were running in all directions. I had to duck to avoid having my head cut off. I remember running, my pole still in hand, and then I woke up.

It wasn't until years later that I recognized the crescent moon shaped metal piece atop our poles was a sickle, and the Lord was speaking to me about the importance of holding onto my faith during difficult times.

Even as a child, I knew these dreams weren't caused by eating too many Gummi Bears before bedtime. They were from God. He was using dreams to reveal Himself to me. These dreams taught me at an early age God was real and involved in my life.

As I grew older, God began expanding the ways He spoke to me or at least expanding my understanding of the ways He spoke. I would read Scriptures that penetrated my soul, have a conversation with a friend that would ring through my spirit, or encounter a situation that reminded me of God's presence.

During my teen years, I wasn't always a poster child for Christianity. By the end of my freshman year of college, I had wandered away from God, but He never wandered away from me. I attended a Christian conference the summer before my sophomore year. I was away from God, and I was miserable. I remember laying my face in my Bible one afternoon and crying out to God. I heard Him speak clearly within my being, *"You are My child, and I have not forgotten you. I love you. You are Mine. You are not your own. Come back to me."* I heard the invitation of God and responded.

Over the next few years of college, a transformation began taking place. Alcohol was no longer my social lubricant and boyfriends no longer determined my personal worth and value. A hunger for God was birthed in my heart, and it has been growing ever since. God's whisper in my spirit—*"You are Mine, you are not your own"*—continues to resonate in my being. His words were a turning point in my life, and He continues to speak, not only at turning points but also in everyday situations.

God still uses dreams to speak to me, but He also uses Scripture, peace, circumstance, and numerous other ways to get my attention and draw my heart back to Him.

I am not anyone special. I am very ordinary. I usually forget where I park my car when I go into the grocery store. I rarely remember to put my socks on before my pants. And those embarrassing stories where the dryer sheet sticks to your clothes—yep, I've got those, too.

Hearing from God isn't designed for special people or only a select few. It's for every believer.

God speaks for a number of reasons, and many of them reveal something about His character. God's words may uncover something about His role as Father, Shepherd, King, Bridegroom, or Teacher. He speaks for a myriad of reasons.

## CONVICTION

God longs for your righteousness. He longs for your purity. He longs for your freedom. He longs for these things even more than you do. And He will gently correct, reprove, and remind you when you stray. Though the word isn't used frequently in Scripture, "conviction" is a major theme found throughout the Bible. God uses the Holy Spirit and His Word to awaken the inborn sense of conscience.

Experiencing conviction is not always pleasant, but it flows out of the Father's love: "For they disciplined us for a short time at their pleasure, but he disciplines us for our good, that we may share his holiness. For the moment all discipline seems painful rather than pleasant; later it yields the peaceful fruit of righteousness to those who have been trained by it" (Hebrews 12:10-11, RSV).

God's correction is actually a blessing in disguise: "Blessed is the man whom God corrects; so do not despise the discipline of the Almighty" (Job 5:17). Think about it. Have you ever been around anyone's children who haven't been disciplined? They are often referred to as "spoiled brats" or "little tyrants" whenever their parents are out of earshot. Those kids can be miserable to be around. Why? Because they haven't been disciplined. They haven't been taught right from wrong or good behavior from misconduct.

Just as a good father disciplines his children for their good, so our heavenly Father disciplines us for our good. Deuteronomy 8:5 says, "Know then in your heart that as a man disciplines his son, so the LORD your God disciplines you."

Those moments of discipline or correction will often come at the oddest times. I remember a particularly rough day. What began as a bad hair day turned into an all around bad day. It was one of those days when you want to kick the cat when no one is looking. I'm sure you've had them.

At the end of a long afternoon, I laced up my tennis shoes and headed out the door for a little exercise and time with God. In reality, I needed to vent. I spent most of the two-mile trail around my home expressing an entire grocery list of "concerns" (the Christian term for complaints) to God. I poured out my heart in a thirty-minute gripe fest. As I rounded one of the last turns toward my driveway, I ran out of things to say and closed with something that resembled more of a "So there!" than an "Amen."

I can still remember carefully watching the pebbles on the paved road—that often acted like ball bearings beneath my feet—to make sure I didn't take a tumble. Focused on the ground, I heard an internal voice—so loud and clear it could have been mistaken for audible—say, *"It's not about you."*

In four little words, God spoke a chapter. Suddenly, the light flipped on, the gray cloud lifted, and the emotional fog burned away. All of my concerns and complaints were centered on one person: me. In my hurt and frustration, I became completely self-consumed and self-focused. God was right; it wasn't about me. It was about Him. In fact, everything is about Him.

I spent the next few days allowing these four words to roll over in my mind and spirit. I felt convicted and repented for my selfishness and pride. I repented for becoming so self-consumed that it bordered on self-worship—placing myself above God in my own mind.

That bad day has long come and gone, but the correction God whispered in my heart is still with me and often revisits on other bad days. Those words will ring through my mind as a wake-up call when I find myself frustrated, discouraged, and even despondent.

As you begin to recognize words of correction or conviction as a gift, then you will begin to welcome them in your life. While the wrapping of conviction may not always be attractive, what is inside will enrich you—a deeper relationship with Him. If you respond to the conviction by repenting and changing your attitude and actions, you can't help but become more like Jesus.

## REVELATION

You are bombarded with thousands of advertisements, sound bites, and pieces of information every day: some you retain, but most you discard. When God gives you a revelation—whether it's about Himself, His Word, or His creation—it usually contains such a bright light of eternal truth you can't help but hold it near your heart. Information may pass, but revelation stays.

God delivers revelation in a multitude of ways. A friend may say something that uncovers a whole new realization for you. A pastor may shed new light on a Bible story during a sermon. A book may uncover truths you didn't realize were hidden.

Don't get me wrong. A moment of revelation isn't necessarily super-spiritual. It may sound big, but it is meant to be normal. Have you ever been reading the Scripture and a particular verse pops off the page, and you recognize a truth you haven't seen before? Suddenly, it becomes alive in your heart and you can't help but mull it over in your mind and return to it. If so, then you have received revelation from God. Simply put, revelation is any of those "Eureka!" moments, when you suddenly see something in the Bible or about God you have never recognized before.

Revelation is one way God communicates with us. Isaiah 55:8-9 says, "'For my thoughts are not your thoughts, neither are your ways my ways,' declares the LORD. 'As the heavens are higher than the earth, so are my ways higher than your ways and my thoughts than your thoughts.'"

First Corinthians 2:10-12 says, "But God has revealed it to us by his Spirit. The Spirit searches all things, even the deep things of God. For who among men knows the thoughts of a man except the man's spirit within him? In the same way no one knows the thoughts of God except the Spirit of God. We have not received the spirit of the world but the Spirit who is from God, that we may understand what God has freely given us."

Often revelation is like a jack-in-the-box. It springs out of nowhere when we least expect it. A young woman named Terry was lying in bed one night when she received a whisper of revelation from the Lord. In her words, here's what happened:

> One night I had an experience I've never had before or since, for no reason at all that I can think of. And it was wonderful. Lying in bed, I suddenly felt the overwhelming love of God. All I could do was whisper loving things back to Him, quietly so I wouldn't wake my husband. This went on for about

twenty minutes. The intense love lifted and I heard in my mind the quiet comment, *"Mary was a single mother, you know."*

I had never thought of Mary that way, and then the quiet voice said, *"I gave her to John because I knew he was the one apostle who would not die."*

I nearly fell out of bed. Who but Jesus would know that? Jesus gave Mary to John when He was at the cross. "Behold thy mother ... behold thy son ..." And history shows us John was indeed the one disciple who lived to old age, so she was cared for until the end of her days.

At church the next day, I shared this with all the young single moms. I encouraged them that just as surely as Jesus had taken care of Mary, He would take care of them.

Terry was able to use this revelation to encourage other believers. Sometimes a revelation is designed specifically for you and some times it is meant to be shared with others. Revelations are a lot like treasures; they can become wonderful finds along your Christian journey.

It is a good idea to pray for revelation—especially when you're sitting down to read the Bible. Ask God to reveal something fresh about His character, His ways, or His truth to you. Listen for His response.

## INTERCESSION

Sometimes God speaks to reveal something about someone else or another situation. He may reveal future promises or blessings. He may also show you a friend's issue, a leader's weakness, an institute's mismanagement, or a governing body's injustice. This is one of the hardest times to hear God speak.

While God may reveal the information, He may not give you the authority or permission to tell others. You have been entrusted with the information for one reason: He is inviting you to pray.

He is not calling you to gossip. He is not asking you to share the revelation with ten people. He is not giving you the okay to tattle-tale. He is simply asking you to pray. It may be for days, weeks, months, or even years. When God reveals information, you need to recognize it as an invitation to spend time on your knees.

Sometimes God may reveal something He is going to do and wants you to be part of praying it through. My friend Sheila couldn't believe the news: One of the pastor's sons in her town was in a terrible car accident. The young man suffered a blow to the head and had permanent brain damage—the two sides of his brain separated during impact.

Before Sheila could begin processing the information, a small phrase dropped into her spirit, *"I hold the keys."* She recognized the Bible reference, "I am the Living One; I was dead, and behold I am alive for ever and ever! And *I hold the keys* of death and Hades" (Revelation 1:18, emphasis added).

From the phrase and corresponding Scripture, an unexplainable confidence encompassed her: the boy would not die. Over the next two weeks, she felt compelled to pray for him. During her times of prayer the words, "Wake up, Jerrod. Wake up," would naturally roll off her lips.

Sheila felt compelled to visit the pastor's son in the hospital. He was in a secured ward, with only family members allowed, but for some strange reason Sheila was permitted into the room. She felt led to anoint his head with oil and pray against death. There was no noticeable response. Sheila returned home.

That night Jerrod woke up. After a few weeks, he was released from the hospital. His brain had been miraculously healed.

Within the next few months, he regained his strength and recovered completely.

Sheila didn't share with the boy's family what the Lord had spoken to her until after he was healed. She knew her role was simply to pray with faith that God would heal him.

Intercession is standing in the gap or asking on behalf of someone else. Ezekiel 22:30 describes the Lord looking for someone who would "build up the wall and stand before me in the gap on behalf of the land" so He would not have to destroy it. God looks for people to pray and become a part of what He is doing. Are you willing?

### GUIDANCE

God often speaks to His people to provide direction. Throughout the Scripture, there are countless references to God guiding His people, and the shepherd-like nature of God is revealed. God is referred to as a shepherd in Genesis 48:15 and 49:24. In John 10:11, Jesus describes Himself as "the Good Shepherd" and Peter refers to Christ as "Shepherd" twice (1 Peter 2:25 and 1 Peter 5:4). In Hebrews 13:20, Jesus is recognized as "the Great Shepherd of the sheep."

There are more than 750 references to sheep in the Bible, and God's people are often referred to as sheep. If you understand the nature of these woolly creatures, it begins to make sense why God would choose to make this comparison. *Nelson's Illustrated Bible Dictionary* explains:

> By nature, sheep are helpless creatures. They depend on shepherds to lead them to water and pasture, to fight off wild beasts, and to anoint their faces with oil when a snake nips them from the grass. Sheep are social animals that gather in flocks, but they tend to wander off and fall into a crevice or get caught in a thorn bush. Then the shepherd

must leave the rest of his flock to search for the stray. Jesus used this familiar picture when He described a shepherd who left 99 sheep in the fold to search for one that had wandered off. The God of the Hebrews revealed His nurturing nature by speaking of himself as a shepherd (Psalm 23). [5]

God's role as shepherd reveals His constant involvement in our lives:

- Psalm 25:9 says, "He guides the humble in what is right and teaches them His way."

- Exodus 15:13 reminds, "In Your unfailing love You will lead the people You have redeemed."

- Isaiah 58:11 promises, "that the Lord will continually guide you" (NAS).

- Psalm 49:11 speaks of God's involvement, "For such is God, Our God forever and ever; He will guide us until death" (NAS).

God rarely shares all the details of life's journey. God shared His long-term plans of blessing with Abraham, but few specifics on how He was going to accomplish it. Guidance was given to many biblical figures, including Joseph, Moses, and Paul on a need-to-know basis. Don't be surprised if God waits until the last minute to reveal His plan to you.

Corrie ten Boom's father explained this principle to her at a young age using a train ticket. The WWII concentration camp survivor describes the moment in her book, *The Hiding Place*:

Father sat down on the edge of the narrow bed. "Corrie," he began gently, "when you and I go to Amsterdam—when do I give you your ticket?"

I sniffed a few times, considering this.

"Why, just before we get on the train."

"Exactly. And our wise Father in heaven knows when we're going to need things, too. Don't run out ahead of Him, Corrie." [6]

You don't need to run ahead of Him either. Ask for His guidance, and trust He will provide it.

God is a hands-on God. He isn't shocked or dismayed by your need for guidance. He is prepared to lead you. He knows you need Him. If you are in rough waves, He wants to lead you to still waters. If you are in a valley, He wants to take you to green pastures. If you are exhausted and weary, He wants to restore your soul. He is ready to take you to the place you need to be.

When God whispers a word of guidance, it may take you on surprising paths or adventures. It may also prevent you from falling off a cliff or wandering away from His perfect will.

A young woman named Ann heard God whisper a word of guidance when she needed it most, but it wasn't the word she expected. When the original call came, the young woman was thrilled. She knew it was a huge opportunity that promised to open more doors in her career path.

She had been struggling to find steady work—waiting for the big break—when a major company called and asked her to be their publicist. It was the perfect offer. She would simply write press releases and follow up with publications to get the company coverage. Ann could work from home and was guaranteed a monthly retainer that would take the pressure off from having to find additional work.

Ann knew the company well and believed in their mission. She contacted the various companies she already worked with to ensure there wasn't any conflict of interest and they all gave her the green light. Everything seemed to be falling into place, but she needed the assurance this was God's will.

On the surface, everything looked fine, but something inside Ann's heart needed an extra measure of certainty. She began to pray, "God, I don't want to be out of Your will. Please speak to me. Everything looks great, but I just want to be sure this is You."

Ann didn't hear anything. Not a peep. The company called the next day and said they would need an answer by the end of the week. Ann continued to pray. The day before she had to make a decision, Ann was going about her house chores when a clear but inaudible voice spoke to her: *"Do you want bronze?"*

She paused. She knew the thought did not come from her own mind and was puzzled by the odd question. Again, the question flooded her mind, *"Do you want bronze?"* Though the words were more of a riddle than a question, she recognized the source. "If this is you, God, then I need to know what You're asking," she prayed. "I don't understand." She didn't hear anything, but over the next few hours the message became clear in her heart, *"Do you want bronze or are you willing to wait for gold?"* She knew what God was asking her.

She thought about both types of metal. Bronze and gold look a lot alike. To the untrained eye, it's possible to mistake them. For those in search of something with real value, bronze is only a distraction.

When the company called the next day, Ann told them she had decided to turn down the position; she was willing to wait for God's best. Some time later while reading through Isaiah she stumbled upon a verse that reminded her she had made the right decision: "Then you will know that I, the LORD, am your Savior, your Redeemer, the Mighty One of Jacob. *Instead of bronze I will bring you gold"* (Isaiah 60:16-17, emphasis added).

## COMFORT

In addition to being a Father and Shepherd, God is also "the Father of compassion and the God of *all* comfort who comforts us in *all* our troubles, so we can comfort those in any trouble with the comfort we ourselves have received from God" (2 Corinthians 1:3-4, emphasis added).

God knows your need to be comforted. He knows you need to be reminded regularly you are not alone or forgotten. You need a pick-me-up. You need to be held. You need to be encouraged. God gives of Himself to comfort you.

Often, God's words of comfort will come when you need them most. They will arrive just after you thought was the nick of time already passed. You know them: Those moments in life when you have hit rock bottom and discovered there was further to fall or reached the end of your rope and found (much to your frustration) an extension.

God knows your breaking point. He is familiar with your maximum. It has been said God will never give you more than you can bear, but the truth is He will never give you more than He can bear. And it can get pretty rough along the way. That is why God is gracious enough to whisper words of comfort.

He understands. Hebrews describes it almost poetically: "For we do not have a high priest who is unable to sympathize with our weaknesses, but we have one who has been tempted in every way, just as we are" (Hebrews 4:15).

If you examine the moments in the Bible where God provides comfort, you will begin to recognize the pleasure He takes in comforting His people.

Listen to the words of Isaiah 51:3: "The LORD will surely comfort Zion and will look with compassion on all her ruins; he will make her deserts like Eden, her wastelands like the garden of the

LORD. Joy and gladness will be found in her, thanksgiving and the sound of singing."

The Lord could simply have looked at Zion with compassion, but He goes on to comfort, redeem, and restore. He places His own gladness and joy in her midst.

Author and speaker Michael Broome tells the story of a missionary doctor who had faithfully served forty years in the remote villages of Africa. When he finally decided to retire, he wired a message ahead and provided the date and time of arrival to the States.

While crossing the sea, he thought of the large homecoming awaiting him in America. He had served countless people in Africa over the years, and while his heart still beat with those people, he knew it was time to return home.

As the ship pulled into port, the missionary's heart leaped with expectation as he scanned the docks. A large crowd of people were gathered, and a huge sign read, "Welcome Home." It was going to be quite a homecoming. But as the man stepped onto shore, he realized the crowds had not gathered for his return but for a movie star who was aboard the same ship.

It was everything he could do to hold back the tears. No one was there to welcome him home. The crowd finally began to disperse. Looking toward heaven, the man half-cried and half-prayed, "God, after giving all those years of my life to my fellow man, was it too much to ask that one person—just one person—be here to welcome me home?'

In the still quiet of his soul, he heard God whisper, *"You're not home yet. When you come home to Me, you will be welcomed."*[7]

## TO GIVE YOU A PEEK INTO THE FUTURE

At times, God will allow you to know something that is going to happen. He may whisper to give you a hope, warning, promise, or an invitation to pray. He may want to give you a glimpse into something that will take place a month, a year, a decade, or even centuries away.

Recall the books of Daniel and Revelation. Both are filled with descriptions of events that would take place hundreds and even thousands of years after the men received the visions.

Many of those in the body of Christ with a gift of prophesy are given glimpses into what is to come. It may be something God wants to do in a certain area or among a particular group of people. Fortunately, it isn't just prophets who God whispers to about upcoming events. In John 15:15, Jesus declared, "I no longer call you servants, because a servant does not know his master's business. Instead, I have called you friends, for everything that I learned from my Father I have made known to you."

As followers of Christ, He is still making the Father's business known to us. He wants us to be a part of what He is doing. Sometimes He lets us know so we will be assured He is involved in what is coming.

During World War II, Corrie ten Boom became a leader of the Resistance in Holland—saving countless Jews from the horrors of Nazi Germany. With numerous underground workers visiting her family's small watch shop, she knew it was only a matter of time before the Nazi soldiers discovered their secret work.

While praying one night, Corrie records a scene that came into her mind. She could see the local market and town hall. A strange, old-fashioned farm wagon came into the town pulled by four huge black horses. In the wagon, she could see herself among other family members, strangers, and friends. They were being drawn across the town square, but no one could get off the wagon. No one wanted to make the journey. In fright, the vision ended.

She cried out for her sister, Betsie, and proceeded to describe the strange scene to her. Corrie records Betsie's response: "(Her) finger traced a pattern on the wooden sink worn smooth by generations of ten Booms. 'I don't know,' she said softly. 'But if God has shown us bad times ahead, it's enough for me that He knows about them. That's why He sometimes shows us things, you know—to tell us that this too is in His hands.'"[8]

Within a short time, Corrie, along with family and friends, were arrested and carted to the concentration camp as she described in the scene.

## TO SHARE WITH OTHERS

Sometimes God speaks because He wants to reveal something to you so you, in turn, will reveal it to someone else. God may whisper a Scripture or life lesson to you in the morning because He wants you to share it with someone else in the afternoon. Someone may need to be encouraged or challenged in their own walk, and God has entrusted you to share His message.

While speaking at a church in New England, author and speaker Lee Grady began giving some prophetic words to specific individuals in the congregation. He describes:

> The second person I called out was a young, college-aged guy on the front row who had blond dreadlocks. I knew nothing about this guy. I had never met anyone in the church before. But the Lord gave me some detailed information about him and word of encouragement.

> I told him he was a worshipper of God, but also a warrior. I told him I saw him and his friends going into churches in the area, and they were doing music events there. I told him the music was very loud and very offensive to some people, but that God was in it—it was a form of spiritual warfare. I told him some churches would invite him in, and they

would actually move the pews out of the church so these events could happen. And the result would be that the enemy would be trampled.

When I finished this word many people cheered. It was obvious they knew something about this guy that I didn't know. When the meeting was over, this guy came over to me. He handed me a CD and explained that he is the lead singer in a Christian alternative band. That was cool enough—to know the Lord had shown me all this stuff about his music when I did not know he was a musician.

But what was more awesome was that I found out from the pastor later that this young man had been involved in doing some worship events at the church, but he had been losing invitations to perform because some people didn't like his dreadlocks. The pastor told me that because of the word, they are "revisiting the issue."

## JUST BECAUSE

Sometimes God speaks just because He loves you. He is not trying to get you to do anything, change anything, or say anything. There are times God speaks simply because He wants to talk to you. He wants to share His heart with you. He wants to affirm you in His love. He wants you to know how close He is to you.

Think of a really kind note you have received from someone. Maybe it's tucked away in a file or an old shoebox. How did it make you feel when you read it?

Now, imagine if the person who wrote the note was sitting across a small table from you looking into your eyes and saying those same things? Which would warm your heart more? The note is wonderful, but when someone takes the time to speak those words to you it is naturally more intimate and endearing.

The "just because" moments reveal the bridegroom nature of God. He is the passionate lover of His people and the Church. He is constantly pursuing and seeking those who are His.

When Adam and Eve were stripped of the Garden, they were not the only ones who missed the intimate communion: God missed it, too. He has been pursuing a close relationship with His people ever since.

Kelly remembers one of those "just because" moments. She was reading a book on a flight home. The way the plane turned in the clouds, the light caught her eye. Looking into the expanse, she heard the Lord whisper, "*I love you.*" The words were as clear as if the gentleman next to her whispered them in her ear. She could feel God's love and sensed His presence.

God didn't say anything else. He didn't correct, instruct, or challenge her. He wasn't trying to get her to do anything; He just wanted her to know how much she was loved.

He wants you to know how much you are loved, too. Don't be surprised if He whispers sweet words in your ear from time to time.

"I have treasured the words
of his mouth more than my
daily bread."

—Job 23:12

# where the whispers begin

You can hear God anywhere. Your home. Your workplace. Your car. Some people hear from God throughout the day while others are more likely to hear Him at a particular time of day. Some people find God speaking anywhere, while others find it helpful to have a certain place where they can meet with Him.

My friends all have different places where they regularly hear from God. Kaley hears from the Lord while she nestles in prayer beside her bed. Ryan hears from God while he worships. Jen hears from God out in the wilderness.

Where do you hear from God? Ideally, the answer is anywhere. But it's also wonderful to have a place where you can turn off the cell phone, unplug the laptop, and get away from the constant demands and distractions of life so you can simply seek God. Jesus seemed to prefer mountaintops. What do you prefer?

If you don't already have one, you need to find a place where you can get quiet and hang with God. Ideally, it needs to be someplace close and readily accessible. A spot that is a three-hour drive may be great for a retreat, but you need to have a place where you can visit daily, a place where He can speak to you.

When you get there, you need to have a few things handy: a Bible, a notebook or journal, a pen, CD player, and a few worship albums.

How do you begin to hear and recognize God's whispers? Four basic principles are involved in the journey of learning to hear God's voice: seek, listen, be patient, and obey.

## A SEEKING HEART

Did you ever play hide and seek as a child? Maybe you played with kids in the neighborhood or your best friend. You would each take a turn running around, tucking yourself into brambly shrubs, the corner of the attic behind a box or under the kitchen sink. It was always more fun to be the person hiding. But if you were the seeker, you knew there were only so many places to look. After searching for the neighbor kid in the yard, under the bed, and in the shower, you found him in his favorite spot: behind the stairs.

In a similar way, God plays hide and seek with us. There are times He will draw near. You can sense His presence. You can feel the tugging at your heart. He has found you! Other times, He will tuck Himself behind a truth, a person or a difficult situation, and it is your job to find Him then.

Seeking is an ongoing process. First Chronicles 16:11 exhorts, "Look to the LORD and his strength; seek his face always."

In the Old Testament, David was a seeker. Something within him compelled him toward the Lord. His desire for God became greater than his physical desires. In Psalm 63, David wrote, "O God, you are my God, earnestly I seek you; my soul thirsts for you, my body longs for you, in a dry and weary land where there is no water." The wording within the verse is so strong, if it were altered slightly, it could be used for an Obsession perfume ad. David craved God. He hungered and thirsted for his Creator, and this desire was extremely pleasing to the Lord.

God rewards those who seek or pursue Him. The Bible admonishes us to seek God, and God promises a great reward for those who engage in the quest: Himself. Deuteronomy 4:29 promises, "But from there you will seek the Lord your God, and you will find Him if you search for Him with all your heart and all your soul."

God places an intrinsic value in seeking Him. Humans tend to want quick, clear, concrete answers. We want to find out what to do, do it, and be done. We lose sight of the fact there isn't anything God can't do Himself. He is not as concerned with "doing the stuff" as He is in relationship.

I remember solving story problems in math class. Two trains, 100 miles apart, travel toward each other at different speeds. Based on the time the two trains departed, what time would they meet? For extra credit, I had to figure out the mile marker where they would pass.

All I really wanted was a train ticket out of the class, but since no one offered I had to settle for getting some friends to help me with the problem. I wanted the right answer so I could move on to something else. Now I realize the core of the lesson wasn't really about trains, speeds, or even math skills (which I still don't use): it was learning how to think.

In the same way, God's interest lies in our seeking to know Him. Sometimes He'll hold back an answer or response so we will continue seeking. Instead of offering an answer, sometimes He offers His hand. He stretches it out and offers to walk beside us.

In addition to seeking, dependence is also important to God. The Father often communicates a general direction that will make you think and become more dependent on Him. For example, when God told to Abraham His offspring would number more than the stars, it seemed impossible. At the time, Abraham was without any children, and the promise must have made him wonder: How is

God going to do it?

God never told Abraham. He just did it.

As a young man, Joseph was given a dream he would one day be higher in prominence than his brothers and father. Again, God never told "little Joe" how He was going to do it (which was probably a good thing).

He just did it.

God never told the prophets exactly how He was going to redeem mankind. He whispered more than 300 prophecies about a Messiah, but when an angel stood at the foot of a young virgin's bed with the good news, she was as surprised as anyone.

If you want to begin hearing God's voice, you need to seek Him and recognize your dependence on Him. When you begin seeking God, you are going to need to initiate a conversation through prayer and ask God to speak to you. Be honest with Him. Tell Him any frustrations, fears, or doubts you may have about hearing from Him. Admit your need for Him. Confess your disappointments with Him. Ask Him to give you ears to hear and eyes to see the ways in which He is speaking. Ask Him for the ability to discern His voice from your own.

The right prayer is the one that comes naturally from your heart. It is okay if you aren't poetic or if you stumble over your words. Don't try to be religious. Be yourself. Be real. It might go something like this:

*God,*

*I want to know You. I want to hear You. I want to have Your presence awakened in my life so I can hear Your words and obey. I ask that You speak to me. Give me ears to hear You and eyes to recognize how You're at work in my life. Help me to discern Your voice from the many voices of the world. And please confirm to me what You're saying. I want to have a vibrant relationship with You.*

*In Jesus' name. Amen.*

In your seeking, be confident He sees and hears you. Yes, God whispers, but He also listens to the whispers of your heart. Psalm 65:2 reflects on God's willingness to lend an ear, "O you who hear prayer, to you all men will come." Never forget "The eyes of the LORD are on the righteous and his ears are attentive to their cry" (Psalm 34:15).

## A BIBLICALLY-BASED HEART

One of the most common ways God speaks is through His Word. Hebrews 4:12-13 describes the Word of God as "living" and "active." It is sharper than any two-edged sword with the ability to judge thoughts and even attitudes of the heart.

If you want to know God and His voice, then you need to spend time in His Word. It's God's megaphone for speaking to His people. If you don't know the Bible reasonably well, then you may not hear as quickly, clearly, or with as much certainty. The Scriptures serve as a rudder when you are listening to God. They provide balance, confirmation, and direction. The Scriptures will also help you sort through the whispers you think might be from Him.

Many times verses or passages of the Bible are the actual whisper. God will speak a Scripture directly to you from a passage. For example, you may be reading Jesus' Sermon on the Mount and stumble across Matthew 5:9: "Blessed are the peacemakers, for they will be called sons of God." In this verse, Jesus is speaking to the crowd, but when you read the words, you recognize that Jesus is speaking directly to you. It may be a general word or something that speaks very specifically into your life. Maybe God is telling you to reconcile a situation or friendship. Maybe He is confirming something He's already echoed in your heart.

You may be reading and find a person in the Bible in a similar situation to the one you are in. Or you may have a particular issue on your mind. A list of Scriptures on the subject can illuminate God's heart for the topic.

God will regularly use the Bible to speak to you. Therefore, a major part of listening to God is spending time reading the Bible. Get to know it. Memorize passages. Store up God's word in your heart. It will protect you from being led astray or falling into sin. Deuteronomy 11:18-21 instructs:

> "Fix these words of mine in your hearts and minds; tie them as symbols on your hands and bind them on your foreheads. Teach them to your children, talking about them when you sit at home and when you walk along the road, when you lie down and when you get up. Write them on the doorframes of your houses and on your gates, so that your days and the days of your children may be many in the land that the LORD swore to give your forefathers, as many as the days that the heavens are above the earth."

You will find that those portions you studied and learned will pop into your mind in various situations and throughout the day. This is a healthy, normal part of the Christian life. In John 14:26 Jesus promises "the Counselor, the Holy Spirit, whom the Father will send in my name, will teach you all things and will remind you of everything I have said to you."

God's word is to be savored. Allow your mind to marinate in passages and Bible stories throughout the day. Take the portions you read during your quiet times with you. Look for Him to continue to reveal things through them.

Recently, I was reading the story of Noah. Genesis 7:11-12 caught my attention: "In the six hundredth year of Noah's life, on the seventeenth day of the second month—on that day all the springs of the great deep burst forth, and the *floodgates of the heavens* were opened. And rain fell on the earth forty days and forty nights" (emphasis added).

Water literally covered the land until every mountaintop was covered. Now that's a lot of water! The phrase "floodgates of heaven" is little unusual, and I remembered another place in the Bible where the term is used. Malachi 3:10 reads: "'Bring the whole tithe into the storehouse, that there may be food in my house. Test me in this,' says the LORD Almighty, 'and see if I will not throw open the *floodgates of heaven* and pour out so much blessing that you will not have room enough for it'" (emphasis added).

When God threw open the floodgates of heaven for Noah, water fell for forty days and nights. When God throws open the floodgates of heaven—releasing blessing—for those who are faithful and generous in giving, can you imagine how much blessing is poured forth? It's staggering. The connection between these two verses was a precious encouragement for me to continue being faithful in generosity. The more time I spend reading the Bible and reflecting on its passages, the more likely I am to receive these little verses of encouragement.

If you aren't familiar with the Bible and you're looking for a place to begin, consider the book of John. Find a Bible translation you can understand and pick one that has the words of Jesus printed in red. Read through the book of John once and then begin going through it a second time at a slower pace.

Reflect on the words Jesus used and the messages He delivered. Note the issues He chose to address during His short time in ministry. What did He applaud? What disappointed Him? How did He interact with people? Look at Jesus' words and life and be open to what He may be speaking to you through the Scriptures.

As you study the Bible, you will become more familiar with it. More importantly, you will become more familiar with God and His heart. Even without hearing a specific whisper from the Lord, you will naturally know what pleases Him. Sometimes without even asking Him, the answer will be there. You will know God's will or how Christ would respond.

It may help your study to put verses to music and create songs to help memorize passages. Or you may find it helpful to copy portions on portable three- by five-inch cards to carry with you. You may want to tape Scripture portions on your bathroom mirror or refrigerator door.

Bible teacher Joy Dawson suggests writing out whole sections of the Word. Remember that the purpose of studying the Bible isn't to know about God but to know Him. As you read passages and stories, reflect on the questions: What does this say about God? What does this say about His personality? His character? His likes and dislikes? Ask God how you can use this revelation to become more like Him.

## AN INQUIRING HEART

In addition to studying the Scriptures, consider asking God questions. This may seem simple, but asking God a question implies humility and dependency. King David discovered this at an early age. Throughout 1 and 2 Samuel, he would regularly inquire of the Lord, and the Lord would speak to him.

Sometimes he would inquire through one of the priests and at other times he would inquire directly. Often his questions circled around battles he was about to face. Would the Israelites win? How should they attack?

David knew he could never inquire of the Lord too much. Like David, you may be facing a major decision in your life. If so, it's time to inquire of the Lord. You may have a strained relationship with a friend or family member. It's time to inquire of the Lord. You may have a Scripture you don't understand. It's time to inquire of the Lord.

Ask Him to give you insight. Ask Him to reveal things that are hidden. Ask Him to show you how to pray. Ask Him what you should be learning from the situation. Ask Him to reveal the real meaning or truth to you. Ask. And keep asking.

Many people find it helpful to record their prayers and inquiries in a notebook or journal. You may want to ask questions such as:

- What is stopping my friend from becoming a Christian?

- Why is there so much friction between a family member and me?

- How can You bring about good in this situation?

- Where are You leading me?

- What are You trying to say in this chapter of the Bible?

- When are You going to allow this situation to change?

In addition to asking God about life issues, I also ask God about portions of the Bible that I don't understand. I've written little question marks along side of various verses and stories in my Bible that leave me puzzled or seem to have a deeper meaning I can't grasp. I'll search for answers in commentaries and concordances, but there are times even Bible resources leave me wondering. So I record the question mark as a quiet prayer to God that I want to understand more. He hasn't answered all of them, but over the years, I've watched Him provide fresh insight into the Scripture.

After you begin seeking God and spending time with Him and in His Word, then it's time to begin listening for His reply.

## A LISTENING HEART

Think back on your life. Are there any times you felt God convict you about an issue? Have you ever been reading the Bible and a particular verse or passage applied perfectly to circumstances in your life? Have you ever felt compelled to pray for someone, visit someone, or give something to someone seemingly "out of the blue?" Have you ever had an encounter with someone that had one-in-a-million odds?

If so, then God was probably whispering to you. He was convicting, revealing, exhorting, and communicating with you. He was speaking to you! It is important to remember and reflect on these times, because God wants to continue to speak to you in those ways and new ones.

Hearing God's voice requires one central element: listening. While it may sound easy, actually making time to sit still can prove quite challenging in today's super-busy, success-driven world. It is hard to get quiet and even harder to stay there. Prayer often becomes a time of pleading with God, shattered by a "hold on just a sec ..." because the phone rings, there is a knock at the door, the neighbor needs a hammer.

The list goes on.

Hearing from God requires more than just a quiet setting. It requires a quiet heart. It means becoming still enough on the inside despite the craziness that may be going on outside. Psalm 46:10 challenges, "Be still, and know that I am God; I will be exalted among the nations, I will be exalted in the earth."

The command to "Be still" is more difficult than you might think. It requires more than your mouth being closed. It requires your heart being open.

In listening to God, you must become vulnerable. You can't fake it with God. There is no pretending. No masks. Just you and Him. This may be uncomfortable or even difficult at first, but it's worth persevering. It is worth the time and energy to know the One who already knows you and understands.

Most believers have a tendency to talk on and on to God, but they don't stop to listen. It can be a real problem. How can you hear His voice if you are the one doing all the talking? Are you giving God time to speak to you?

Worship can be extremely helpful in transitioning from the busyness of the day to time with God. Music combined with vertical lyrics—those that speak to God rather than just about God—can help you focus and draw your heart toward Him. You may prefer to create your own music with an instrument.

In *Enjoying God*, teacher and author S.J. Hill advises:

> As your mind begins to unwind, start to express words of love and adoration to the Father. You can do it out loud or under your breath. Your words don't have to be complex or even complete sentences. Express your heart to Him. Tell Him what you like about Him. Thank Him for the little things He's done in your life. As you worship, remember He's not out there somewhere in the wild blue yonder. He lives inside you. Your body is His temple. Offer yourself as a resting place for Him, and tell Him you want Him to be your resting place.[9]

As you spend more time with God, you will undoubtedly begin sensing His presence. You may feel a certain peace, confidence or reassurance that He is near you. You may be overwhelmed with a certain aspect of Him—His beauty, love, power, holiness, or goodness. It is important, if at all possible, not to rush those moments. If you allow them, and more importantly Him, to linger, then they will become the highlight of your day.

Ideally, these special moments with God should not be limited to your set apart time with Him. Allow them to spread throughout your daily life. Hill encourages:

> Try to find times throughout the day to steal away with Him. In other words, run away with Him in your heart and mind while you're driving to and from work, riding in an elevator, waiting in the grocery checkout line or working out on a treadmill. The Father is everywhere, and His desire for you is unending. Bring your thoughts around to Him throughout the day. Express your love and adoration. Ask Him to bring you into a deeper awareness of His presence until you find yourself living more and more in an attitude of prayer and worship." [10]

Don't be surprised if you are sensing the presence of God when He begins to talk to you. The Bible says Samuel "grew up in the presence of the LORD" (1 Samuel 2:21). It is interesting to note where Samuel was located when the first whisper from God came: "Samuel was lying down in the temple of the LORD, where the ark of God was" (1 Samuel 3:3). Samuel was next to the ark—a symbol of God's presence—when the LORD called to Samuel.

After you ask God to speak to you, begin spending regular time studying and reflecting on Scripture. Make time to be with Him. Be open to what God is saying to you, and prepare your heart to obey Him.

Missionary Elisabeth Elliot once wrote:

> "The primary condition for learning what God wants of us is putting ourselves wholly at his disposal. It is just here that we are often blocked. We hold certain reservations about how far we are willing to go, what we will or will not do, how much God can have of us or what we treasure. Then we pray for guidance. It will not work. We must begin by laying

it all down—ourselves, our treasures, our destiny. Then we are in a position to think with renewed minds and act with a transformed nature. The withholding of any part of ourselves is the same as saying, "Thy will be done up to a point, mine from there on." [11]

In addition, you need to be sensitive to God's leading and nudges. Learn to pray with your eyes and ears open. Not in the physical sense. It's fine if you close your eyes or bow your head, but once you begin to ask God to speak, expect an answer. Be alert for the various ways in which He may respond.

Like a detective, you need to learn how to spot God's fingerprints: those moments and times that are divinely orchestrated. You may hear a conversation that clarifies what you're feeling or have a thought that comes to mind and just makes sense. You may hear the whisper during a family picnic, in a shopping mall, or while watching a movie. You just never know what way God may choose to reveal His will and ways to you. You may discover God has a lot more to say than you ever imagined.

## A Patient Heart

Nowhere in the Bible does God commit to running on our schedule or fitting into our time frame. We are designed to fit into His. God may answer a prayer within a few minutes or He may wait a few millennia. It is simply up to Him. Philippians 4:6 reminds us, "Be anxious for nothing, but in everything by prayer and supplication with thanksgiving let your request be made known to God."

Developing any good spiritual discipline takes time. It requires a measure of effort and patience. "Since ancient times no one has heard, no ear has perceived, no eye has seen any God besides you, who acts on behalf of those who wait for him" (Isaiah 64:4).

Learning to hear, recognize, and discern the ways in which God speaks isn't a quick work. Waiting is involved. It may take several years before you're completely comfortable with hearing and discerning God's voice. No matter how long it takes, you must have confidence that He has heard your prayers and will respond.

## AN OBEDIENT HEART

In *Experiencing God*, Henry Blackaby and Claude King make a simple, but profound observation, "You cannot stay where you are and go with God at the same time." [12]

Hearing from God is worthless if you don't obey. Some people become so focused on discerning whether or not what they heard was from God that they never take the first step of obedience. They feel that if they don't have 100 percent certainty, then everything will turn into a disaster. The fear of being wrong prevents them from ever having the opportunity to be right.

God is a big God. He can handle it. He knows you are going to stumble and make mistakes. Remember, God looks at the heart. When He sees people stepping out—even if they are heading in the wrong direction—He can lovingly correct or even turn things around to use it for His glory. Think about it. Would you rather stand before God and say, "I wasn't sure it was You, so I didn't do anything," or "*I wasn't sure that it was You, so I stepped out in faith trusting You would correct me if I was wrong*"?

Several years ago I was at the beach with some Christian friends when I noticed a man sitting nearby. As I watched him, my heart began to melt with compassion and I felt this strange sense in my heart that God wanted to do some sort of reconciliation between the man and his siblings. I mentioned to one of my friends that we should go talk to him.

Avoiding the "thus-saith-the-Lord" approach, I opted for the safer,

"How's it going?" and "What's your name?" strategy. The conversation progressed quite naturally, and I finally asked him about his family. When he revealed he was an only child, my heart dropped. I had blown it. I missed God. As my friend continued talking with the man, I quietly prayed, "Sorry, God. I was wrong, but at least I didn't publicly embarrass you." By this point, the conversation began taking on a life of its own and before I knew it, my friend and I had shared the Gospel message with this stranger and invited him to church. As we walked away, I laughed aloud. God really can work all things together for good.

God will probably not begin speaking to you by asking you to deliver a message to the President. He may begin with something simple and small. You may be tucked into bed one night about to fall asleep and you hear the Lord whisper, "Your car headlights are on."

Now you have two choices: Roll over and try to get some rest, or get up and check the car headlights. If you get up and the car headlights are on, then you know you have heard from God. If you get up and discover the lights are off, then there's no harm done.

If you stay in bed and it really was God speaking to you, then you'll not only have a dead battery in the morning, you'll also have missed the opportunity to be obedient.

In *It's All About You, Jesus*, Fawn Parish writes, "Obedience prepares us as well. Have you ever wondered how you could show your love for Jesus in greater ways? Be swift to obey. Obedience is not an option for a genuine disciple. Instant obedience is the fastest way to prove the faithfulness of God." [13]

There are promises of provision and blessing for those who are obedient to the Lord. Take a moment and reflect on Deuteronomy 28:1-6:

If you fully obey the LORD your God and carefully follow all his commands I give you today, the LORD your God will set you high above all the nations on earth. All these blessings will come upon you and accompany you if you obey the LORD your God: You will be blessed in the city and blessed in the country. The fruit of your womb will be blessed, and the crops of your land and the young of your livestock—the calves of your herd and the lambs of your flocks. Your basket and your kneading trough will be blessed. You will be blessed when you come in and when you go out.

There are rich rewards for the obedient. At one point in Jesus' ministry a woman in the crowd cried out, "Blessed is the mother who gave you birth and nursed you." To which Jesus corrected, "Blessed rather are those who hear the word of God and obey it" (Luke 11:27-28). In a later passage He reminded His people, "If anyone loves me, he will obey my teaching. My Father will love him, and we will come to him and make our home with him" (John 14:23).

Just how important is obedience? Ask the two men who built houses in the parable of the wise man and fool. The only difference between the two was that one listened and obeyed, and the other just listened. After the rain fell, only one house was standing. If you have any doubts as to which one it was, turn to Matthew 7:24-27.

Through obedience, you begin to develop one of the most powerful tools in the Christian faith. I like to call it "The Knower." You have probably heard someone refer to it. You will ask the straight-forward question, "Well, how do you know?" And they will respond with a seemingly less-than-direct, " I just know." Or "I know because I know because I know." Such claims sound ludicrous until you, too, have developed The Knower.

The Knower is the quiet confidence you have heard from God,

and you are liberated in the knowledge of that Truth. The Knower is an internal track record of experiencing God.

Maybe you have recognized God speaking to you through Scripture in the past. When He speaks to you again through Scripture, you are more confident that it is Him. Or maybe you have sensed the need to move somewhere, and you obeyed. After you move, you discover it really was God and His plan for you. Later, when you sense that same need, you are more confident it is God. You know. You can't really explain it to someone. It's internal. Someone may ask you, "How do you know you are supposed to move?" You respond, "I can just sense it inside. I just know."

The Knower is that voice that says you have been down this path before. You recognize the scenery. You have at least a vague idea of where you are going. The more time you spend with God and are obedient to His commands, the more you get to know Him. You become familiar with His ways, His likes, His dislikes.

The Knower is powerful. It is not infallible. Even veteran believers can be wrong. But after awhile, believers develop an ability to hear God's voice and the faith to stand on His Word. The Knower isn't really about what you know but Who you know. You may recognize the circumstances, but you really recognize Him.

"God's voice thunders in marvelous ways; he does great things beyond our understanding."

—Job 37:5

*ways he whispers*

c h a p t e r     f o u r

God is unlimited in the ways He speaks. He can use anything to grab your attention, turn your head, lift your chin, and bring your mind and thoughts back to Him. And He often does.

God is not satisfied with the five, fifteen, or fifty minutes you spend with Him in the morning or evening. Even if you are there for hours, He isn't content being cooped up in the prayer closet all day. He does not want a long-distance relationship; He wants to be with you. He wants to commune with you at home, work, and play. Whether you are driving to the store, taking out the trash, nursing a child, or checking the mail, God is with you, and He will use little things to remind you He is around.

He may use gardening to teach you something about the fruits of the Spirit. He may use waiting for a wave while you are surfing to reveal something about patience. He may use your own children to give you a deeper understanding of dependence. God is limitless in the ways He speaks. So don't be surprised if He uses dirt, water, or even kids to get your attention.

Here are some of the common ways He speaks. If you recognize one or more of these as ways that God speaks to you, then you are going to need to do some additional study. Consider looking up the key word, whether it's "dream," "vision," or "counsel" in a concordance. Find out what the Bible says about it. Follow up by reading books that specifically tackle these subjects in depth.

## SCRIPTURE

Scripture is one of the most common ways God whispers. Have you ever been reading a passage and a certain phrase or verse catches your attention? All the other words on the page seem to pale by comparison. In those few little words, God is revealing something new, exposing a truth in a fresh way or answering one of your prayers. Suddenly, you are challenged. You are encouraged. Or you simply understand. At that moment, He is whispering to you, and He is using His Word to do it.

Hebrews 4:12 says, "For the word of God is living and active. Sharper than any double-edged sword, it penetrates even to dividing soul and spirit, joints and marrow; it judges the thoughts and attitudes of the heart."

Solomon challenged believers to study, memorize, and meditate on God's wisdom in Proverbs when He wrote, "Bind them upon your heart forever; fasten them around your neck. When you walk, they will guide you; when you sleep, they will watch over you; when you awake, they will speak to you" (Proverbs 6:21-22).

God speaks through Scripture. If you want to know His voice, you must spend time in the Bible—reading, thinking, mulling over, and memorizing passages. It is your umbilical cord to the Father. Second Timothy 3:16 says, "All Scripture is inspired by God and *profitable* for teaching, for reproof, for correction, for training in righteousness" (NAS-Updated, emphasis added). To partake of the *profits*, you need to know the Bible.

God can use a particular verse to speak directly into a situation. Matt finally broke free from his homosexual lifestyle. It was a long, arduous journey with many pitfalls, but he knew he had crossed the line: There was no turning back. With his heart warmed by the realities of God's calling and gifting in his life, Matt wanted to enter the ministry.

He thought carefully before filling out the section entitled "testimony" on his Bible college application. He took a deep breath and began responding to the essay question. When he put down his pen, he had filled up two extra sheets of paper. *What will those who read this testimony think? Did I say too much? Did I say enough?* The questions whirled in his mind. Matt pushed down the mounting anxiety, determined to finish the application. He slipped the completed form back into the envelope and headed to the post office.

Later that night the questions returned. *What will they think of me? How many people on campus will know? How will they respond? Will I even be accepted?* Tossed to and fro by feelings of fear and rejection, he tried to go to sleep. It was no use.

He leaned over and turned on the lamp beside his bed. He reached for his Bible and began to pray. A verse flashed through his head: Acts 10:15. He had no idea what it said, so he thumbed through the well-worn pages to find the Scripture. The words jumped off the page: *"Do not call anything impure that God has made clean."* While the passage was admonishing Peter to embrace Gentile believers as well as certain foods, Matt recognized God was speaking directly to him through the verse. The simple message bathed his soul. God had forgiven him and called him clean. Thanking God, he turned off the light and slept sound.

In the spring of 2001, Matt graduated from the Bible college.

## VISIONS

Visions take different forms for different people. Some people literally see open-eyed visions where they are looking at one thing in the natural but see something completely different taking place in the spiritual realm. Other people receive closed-eye visions. It is something they receive in their mind's eye. It isn't seen with physical eyes, but inside the mind. It may sound strange, but most people can picture something in their mind. It is not too hard.

Let me give you an example: Close your eyes for a moment and picture a tree. It has a thick, round trunk and dark green leaves. Can you envision it? That is an example of what many people experience when they have a closed-eye vision.

In the Old Testament, Ezekiel and Daniel both received visions. In the New Testament, accounts of visions can be found in Luke, Acts and Revelation. People continue to receive visions today. A closed-eye vision tends to be more common than an open-eyed vision. God may give you a vision to awaken your heart about Himself or something He is going to do.

Cameron received a vision that changed the course of his life. While visiting a special renewal service at a church in Canada, Cameron's eyes were drawn to the various groups of college-aged and twentysomethings in the congregation. They had traveled from all over the world to attend the church's services. He could sense their spiritual hunger; it was the same hunger he felt in his own heart.

At the end of the service, an altar call invited anyone who wanted to know God's calling on his or her life to respond. As a college student, Cameron couldn't resist the opportunity and headed toward the altar to receive prayer. Nothing profound happened during the prayer time, and the nineteen year old returned to his hotel room to get some rest.

That night Cameron couldn't sleep. The images of the twentysomethings from the service flashed through his mind. They represented a groundswell movement that seemed to be happening around the world. The problem was, it was happening in a highly fragmented way, mainly with individuals or small groups.

But Cameron felt for the movement to realize its full impact, it needed to be unified and have a strong voice. But how would God gather them together?

In his mind's eye, he saw a flight map similar to those found in the back of airplane seats. It was a map of the world, and red dots marked the hotbeds of this new move of hunger for God. The groups of young people had a passion for Jesus but were isolated and didn't know each other. Cameron had a sense God wanted to use him to connect the dots. He wasn't being called into traditional ministry; he was being called to use media to reach his generation.

Cameron was bombarded with thoughts and ideas on how he could use a magazine, website, and book publishing division to reach his generation. His mind raced with specifics: the size and design of the magazine, marketing ideas, a business plan, and even slogans for the company saturated his thoughts.

As ideas flowed, he could see this media being one of the things God would use to connect the dots of what He was saying in this generation. Media could be the national voice this groundswell movement needed. In his mind's eye, Cameron began to see lines connecting all the little dots within the United States and around the world until they completely blanketed the map. It was nearly five a.m. and his mind was still spinning when he finally flipped on the light and wrote the ideas down on a three- by five-inch piece of paper from his Franklin Planner. When he completed making the notes, he turned off the light, climbed back into bed, and immediately fell asleep.

It wasn't until the next day Cameron recognized God had been speaking to him. He realized the thoughts and vision weren't coming out of his own excitement; they were planted by God. He shared the idea with his parents who quickly raised questions and concerns with the business plan. Cameron took their suggestions to heart and further developed the strategies and ideas. During his senior year of college, he took an entrepreneur class where he wrote a business plan for Relevant Media Group.

Over the next six years, Cameron continued to improve the business strategy and plan for the company. In 2000, Relevant Media Group became a reality, and this book is one of the fruits of its publishing division.

## DREAMS

Dreams are similar to visions, except they occur only during sleep. Dreams can be used to offer guidance, direction, comfort, revelation, or any other word God may want to speak.

Throughout the course of your life you will have countless dreams. In some of them, God is speaking and in others He is not. How do you know the difference?

If you have a dream and you are not sure if it's from God, then you need to ask Him. Ask the Lord if He was trying to communicate something to you in your dream. If so, what was He trying to say?

Dreams are not always easy to interpret and they do not always come to pass immediately. One of the famous dreamers of the Bible was Joseph. While he was still a teenager, Joseph had a dream that he was going to be greater than his brothers. Foolishly, he shared the dream with them, and they hated him for it. At one point, Jacob (Joseph's father) rebuked the teenager for his dream even though Scripture reveals he "kept the saying in his mind" (Genesis 37:11, NAS).

Joseph had to wait many years and live through multiple trials—

including slavery, seduction, imprisonment, and neglect—before the dream came true and he became a ruler of Egypt. Joseph probably doubted the validity of the dream and its meaning numerous times, yet God eventually brought it to pass.

If you feel God is trying to communicate with you through a dream, then why not ask Him what the various elements of the dream mean? Why were certain people, objects, words, or even colors used in your dream? Ask the Lord to speak to you through Scripture and those around you.

God will often use symbols and colors to speak in a dream. For example, something green may represent new life. Something dark or black may represent danger or possible harm. Water may represent cleansing. Ask the Lord to reveal what each piece or segment of the dream means.

Record your dream in a journal and wait patiently for God to reveal the meaning. You may want to consider sharing your dream with someone who also hears from the Lord through dreams.

Several years ago, I had a dream about one of my Christian neighbors. In the dream, I saw a golden light fill her home and explode in it until everything was dazzlingly bright. I immediately awoke, turned on the light, recorded the dream, and began asking the Lord what it meant.

In my heart, I knew the gold light represented a large blessing from God. I had an inward sense God was going to bless my neighbor, but I was puzzled by why my neighbor was never in the dream. I asked the Lord what He was intending. Reflecting on the scene, I remembered that the gold light exploded in the home, not on an individual person. A simple thought that was not my own flashed through my mind: "*I am going to bless her household for it is my good pleasure to bless those who are upright and diligently seek Me.*"

The next morning I awoke early and prayed as to whether or not to tell my neighbor. Around nine a.m. I finally had a peace about telling her, but a definite discomfort about sharing something as vague as "I really feel like the Lord is going to bless you, because it is His pleasure to bless His righteous ones."

Though I knew her well, I was nervous and stumbled over my words. It was awkward, but I relayed the dream and closed with several disclaimers including, "This is probably the vaguest message anyone has ever told you."

My neighbor looked at me with a blank face. Then, she smiled. "That's funny," she said. "Because when you knocked I was just hanging up the phone with my sister. My brother is developmentally disabled. It's been a real financial strain on all of us. He just got a letter from the Social Security department saying they have miscalculated his benefits. They're sending him a check for $20,000."

## AUDIBLE AND INTERNAL AUDIBLE

Throughout the Bible, God spoke audibly to His people. Both in the Old and New Testaments, stories abound of God speaking directly and audibly. Few believers today experience the audible voice of God. They are more likely to experience the internal audible voice.

The internal audible voice is like an audible voice, except you do not hear it with your ears. Instead, you hear it with your spirit. The internal audible voice is a thought, phrase, or concept that rings clear within your being. Sometimes the internal audible voice is so clear and bold it almost seems like it is audible.

God will often whisper Scriptures using the internal audible voice. You may be going along and a passage, verse, or Bible story floods your mind. The words of the Scripture take on new meaning in the light of the situation you are in.

You may be praying about a particular issue and you hear the word "go," "no," or "wait" echo in your spirit. You may hear the Lord speak a word of encouragement or correction.

This inward leading is from the Holy Spirit. In John 14:16-18, Jesus promises, "And I will ask the Father, and he will give you another Counselor to be with you forever—the Spirit of truth. The world cannot accept him, because it neither sees him nor knows him. But you know him, for he lives with you and will be in you. I will not leave you as orphans; I will come to you."

Jesus refers to the Holy Spirit as a "Counselor" and the "Spirit of truth." His promise is that the Holy Spirit will live in us and with us. Jesus highlighted this when He said, "If anyone loves me, he will obey my teaching. My Father will love him, and we will come to him and make our home with him" (John 14:23).

God is in you. It should come as no surprise that He will speak to you from within. He will allow His message to resonate inside you, because He lives inside of you.

Patty was going through a particularly rough time. She made a mental list of her closest Christian friends and thought about who to call. One was living in Spain and there was no way to contact her. Another was out of town. Another was difficult to reach. She considered calling a major ministry just to have someone to talk to and pray with. Before she could pick up the phone, she heard an internal audible voice of the Lord say, "*Come unto Me.*"

She recognized the verse; it was Jeremiah 33:3, one that her friends called "God's telephone line." It reads, "Call unto me, and I will answer thee, and will show thee great things, and difficult, which thou knowest not" (ASV). The Lord was inviting her to lean on Him during this difficult time. She responded and was filled with peace.

## SPONTANEOUS IMPRESSIONS

At times you will sense God's leading but not hear anything—audibly or internally. Rather, God is speaking to you through spontaneous thoughts, feelings, and impressions.

Mark Virkler, author of *Communion With God*, describes this form of communication effectively when he writes:

> For example, haven't each of us had the experience of driving down the road and having a thought come to us to pray for a certain person? We generally acknowledge this to be the voice of God calling us to pray for that individual. My question to you is, "What did God's voice sound like as you drove in your car? Was it an inner, audible voice, or was it a spontaneous thought that lit upon your mind?" Most of you would say God's voice came to you as a spontaneous thought.
>
> So I thought to myself, "Maybe when I listen for God's voice, I should be listening for a flow of spontaneous thoughts. Maybe spirit-level communication is received as spontaneous thoughts, impressions, feelings and visions." Through experimentation and feedback from thousands of others, I am now convinced that this is so. [14]

With God thoughts, you know the impression or feeling did not originate with you; it originated with Him. You may be praying about your future and suddenly you find yourself praying for your grandmother. You may be thinking about your job, and you find yourself overwhelmed with compassion for a co-worker who is in need. You may just be listening to the Lord and sense His overwhelming love and compassion pour over you. These out-of-the-blue thoughts and impressions are often from the Father. God will consume your mind with Himself.

Colossians 3:16 challenges, "Let the word of Christ dwell in you richly as you teach and admonish one another with all wisdom, and as you sing psalms, hymns and spiritual songs with gratitude in your hearts to God."

When the words of Christ dwell richly inside you, don't be surprised if you hear His voice echoing in your spirit and mind through thoughts and impressions.

Looking at the large, opulent houses that lined the shores, Marjane smiled with fond remembrance of the beautiful home she had once shared with her husband. It had been two years since they had left their lucrative occupations, sold their golf course home, and invested in a modest sailboat.

Rather than handling real estate transactions and building projects, they were now handing out Bibles to natives of the out islands in the Caribbean. Together, they had quietly taken a step back from the American dream to fulfill a less conventional role as missionaries. It wasn't a position that was applauded or even noticed by most who knew them. They merely had the blessing of their church and a desire to be used by God.

The houses still caught Marjane's eye. Trimmed lawns. Blooming flowers. Docks with boats leisurely nestled before them. There wasn't a house along the rich shoreline priced below a million dollars. She reflected on the simplicity of their lives now and smiled again.

Less than an hour later, the couple docked their boat and headed into the marina's restaurant for a bite to eat. Sitting down, Marjane couldn't help but notice the six well dressed, perfectly manicured ladies sitting at the table across from them. Their clothes were tailored. Large stones rested on their ring fingers while tennis bracelets decorated their wrists. Their make-up was flawless. Their hair was flawless. Their entire outfits were flawless.

"They're perfect," Marjane thought. She reflected on her own life. Looking down, she noticed a small stain on her blouse. Her boat shoes were worn. After the voyage, she hadn't even taken time to put on lipstick. She didn't want to be jealous. She didn't want to regret her decision to leave her business, but the thoughts flooded her mind.

Then, an almost humorous thought that wasn't her own entered her spirit. *"What you're seeing is like a chocolate bunny at Easter. These worldly things may look perfect on the outside, but when you bite in, they're hollow and empty."* Marjane recognized the thought as from the Lord. She reflected on this simple truth. After dinner, she returned to the boat a little bit more content.

## JOURNALING

Journaling is another way of communicating with God. You can write out your fears, frustrations, hopes, and dreams. You can confess sins and find comfort. In a journal, you can ask God questions, make requests, and ask for insight into situations.

A journal can become a sacred place. Mere blank pages are transformed into a site where you can record the most intimate parts of your soul. A place where you can travel with your deepest thoughts and confessions. A place where you can slip off the mask of who you are supposed to be and slip into something more comfortable: who you really are.

God often speaks to people through their journals. Many people read old passages and discover God was actually answering prayers as they poured out their hearts. Some people underline or place quotes around the words they feel God is speaking to them. They may record a Scripture that speaks into a situation or write words faster than the mind can comprehend. Through the pages of a journal, you can hear from God.

In *Spiritual Journaling: Recording Your Journey Toward God,*

Richard Peace writes:

> Journaling is, itself, a spiritual discipline. It focuses mind and heart on the issues of growth with the aim of discerning what God is doing in one's life. By using a journal, we come in touch with our cutting edges of growth, those areas where questions exist or where there is need or longing. These are areas where the Holy Spirit seems most active.
>
> Journaling is also an aid to other spiritual disciplines. Writing down your insights is helpful in Bible study. Writing out prayers helps you to communicate with God. Creating a poem that praises God is an act of worship. [15]

Over time you will begin seeing God answer the prayers, requests, and concerns expressed in your journal. It will be richly filled with testimonies of God's faithfulness.

## CONSCIENCE

Everyone has a conscience, but some are more sensitive than others. Conscience is a person's innate awareness that helps discern between good and evil. It is often a feeling or inward sense. The Holy Spirit often uses conscience to correct and protect, but the conscience is not infallible. Paul writes, "My conscience is clear, but that does not make me innocent. It is the Lord who judges me" (1 Corinthians 4:4).

You will always have the choice as to whether or not to respond to your conscience. Ignoring your conscience can have adverse affects on your moral and spiritual life.

Have you ever seen a western film where a metal triangle was used to call people to dinner? A metal rod is inserted in the triangle and rolled around the edges to create a loud clanking sound. Your conscience is a lot like that triangle. Each time you say or do something that goes against God's best for you, a feeling of uneasiness or guilt alerts you. When you respond by apologizing, repenting, or making things right, your conscience becomes quiet again and a peaceful calm in your spirit returns. But if you repeatedly ignore your conscience, the sound will eventually grow dim. Repeated sin eventually deadens the conscience.

David was known for quickly responding to his conscience. Second Samuel 24:10 records a time when David counted his fighting men, an action born out of lack of trust in God and was "conscience-stricken." He told the Lord, "I have sinned greatly in what I have done. Now, O LORD, I beg you, take away the guilt of your servant. I have done a very foolish thing."

As followers of Jesus Christ, it is important to maintain a pure conscience and help others to do the same. Paul offers an example of this in 1 Corinthians 10:27-29: "If some unbeliever invites you to a meal and you want to go, eat whatever is put before you without raising questions of conscience. But if anyone says to you, 'This has been offered in sacrifice,' then do not eat it, both for the sake of the man who told you and for conscience sake—the other man's conscience, I mean, not yours."

God can use your conscience to speak to you at any time and bring you back to Himself. A young woman named Faith was busy getting ready to go see her boyfriend. She was putting on a cute outfit and thinking about how they would spend the evening together when a verse popped into her mind: "Everything is permissible for me but not everything is beneficial" (1 Corinthians 6:12).

She had read this verse before many times, but suddenly it was alive in her heart. God was speaking to the young woman about her physical relationship with her boyfriend. Things hadn't gotten out of hand, but she knew the Lord was offering a word of caution and correction, and she responded.

## LIFE EXPERIENCES

God is the creator of life, and He loves to invade it. Whether you are at work or on vacation, resting, running, eating, or playing, God can use the simple and mundane as well as the extraordinary to speak. It is important to have your ears and heart open to the Father's voice all the time.

God can even use a pet to reveal something about His nature. Twenty-six-year-old Kaley knew the chances of her cat, Missy, coming back to the house alive were slim. The seventeen-year-old cat was diagnosed with diabetes and kidney failure six months earlier. The doctors gave Missy less than a month to live, but somehow she had found the strength to survive and return home. She was considerably thinner and her fur had long lost its shine, but Kaley didn't seem to notice. She loved her childhood friend and recounted Missy stories to everyone who would listen.

When Missy began getting weak, Kaley took extra time with her. When Missy could no longer sleep in the bed without vomiting, Kaley slept on the floor beside her. When Missy had accidents in the house, Kaley cleaned them up without complaint. When Missy rubbed up against her leg signaling that she wanted to be held, Kaley kept her warm in her arms. Kaley silently hoped and prayed God would allow Missy to die peacefully in her presence.

That is what made this fateful night so difficult. Missy had slipped outside in the cold, wet darkness through an open door. With guests visiting, it was several hours before Kaley even noticed. At three a.m., she began to hunt for Missy around her home and neighborhood. It was pitch black and cold; she began to wonder when the rain would turn to snow. The damp cold pierced through Kaley's winter coat. She began to pray, "Oh God, don't let Missy go. Not like this."

She continued to search for Missy behind bushes, trashcans and under neighbors' cars. She watched a car pass by on the road.

"God, please show me where Missy is," she begged. "Don't let her get hit."

It was four in the morning, and there was still no sign of Missy. Wet and cold, Kaley returned home for a few minutes to get warm. Her praying turned into pleading. "No, God! It can't be like this. I haven't nursed and cared for her for seventeen years for her to freeze to death."

She returned outside. She could not give up. Not while there was a chance Missy was alive. Raindrops pierced her coat. Her footing became unsure as she continued the search. Five o'clock passed. Still no Missy.

Kaley's prayers were moistened with tears. How long could Missy make it in the cold rain? Sometime around six a.m., Kaley began to lose hope. Her prayers circled around one meager word, "Help."

The young woman was not only shivering, but also emotionally and physically exhausted. She had visited every place she could think of twice. Some places three times. She looked again at the road and began to cry. "Oh, God," was all she could plead.

In the cold silence, Kaley heard a calm, warm voice inside her spirit, *"With the same fervor and tenacity that you are searching for Missy, I have been searching for you. Even through the darkness, I continually seek those who are Mine."*

Kaley began to weep. In the darkest hour before the dawn, she was reminded God was with her. He had heard her prayers. And He had allowed her to sense just a small portion of His love and desire for His children. Somehow the simple but profound revelation spoke warmth and hope into her spirit. Kaley continued searching. At eight in the morning, behind a pile of soggy boxes, she heard a soft "meow."

## CIRCUMSTANCE

God speaks through circumstance. Opportunities knock and doors open. They can take the form of an acceptance letter, an invitation, an offer, a gift, or a contract. Doors also shut. A job is not offered. A marriage proposal shunned. Support funds never raised. A clearly displayed "Sold" sign.

God often uses circumstance to direct, guide, teach, and lead. God uses circumstances to speak, but this should by no means be a believer's guide to following God's will. Left to the waves of circumstance, it is too easy to be tossed to and fro among hundreds of possibilities and options.

When you believe God is speaking to you through circumstance, ask Him to confirm it through a different source. One woman discovered God's leading through circumstance and experienced peace as a confirmation.

A newly divorced single mom of a newborn boy and three-year-old daughter found herself trying to keep long hours as a newspaper reporter in a city in Oklahoma, 1,300 miles away from her family. Natalie desperately wanted to pack up the kids and go home to Florida, where she would have the support of her mom and dad and where her kids could grow up with grandparents, aunts, uncles, and cousins.

But Natalie knew she could not leave her job in Oklahoma without a way to support her children. When no newspaper job in Florida immediately appeared on the horizon, Natalie waited. It wasn't easy. She heard no internal voice, no confirmation of any specific direction through dreams, visions, or prophecy.

One afternoon, her mother called her at work and mentioned that the University of South Florida in her hometown was offering large grants to professional journalists who would come to USF to obtain a master's degree in journalism. Natalie shrugged it off, not ever having considered the possibility of going back to school.

Later that same day, Natalie opened the weekly edition of the trade magazine, *Editor & Publisher*, and turned to the classified section, looking for a job. The first listing under the first column was from the University of South Florida, seeking applicants for that journalism grant—and the deadline was that day.

Natalie knew that set of circumstances was more than just coincidence. "Divine coincidence" is what her mother would call it. Natalie placed a call to the number in the ad, connected with a professor and got the application ball rolling. The graduate assistantship she received a couple of weeks later was enough to help her move back to Florida with her children, obtain her master's degree at the school's expense, and have the privilege of watching her children flourish with loving family members around them.

While Natalie still recalls no audible voice telling her what to do, the circumstances made it clear. And the peace she felt in making the decision confirmed it.

## COUNSEL AND OTHERS

In 1 Corinthians 12, the church is described as a human body. It has many members but together they make up one body. Like different organs in a human, different people have different talents and skills; they all need each other. God has not put you in the body of Christ to be a Lone Ranger; He has placed you in the body so you can learn, grow, and be challenged by those around you.

God will often speak through those in authority over you including your parents, spouse, counselors, and friends. It is wise, not weak, to seek counsel.

Sometimes God will use someone with a title to speak to you, and other times He may choose to use a complete stranger. Author

Barbara Johnson tells the story of a woman who was having a par-ticularly rough day: She had overslept and was late for work. Her time in the office wasn't much better and when she finally boarded the city bus home, there wasn't a single seat available. The bus lurched to its standard stops, throwing the exhausted woman in all directions.

The woman heard a man toward the front of the bus declare, "Beautiful day, isn't it?" She couldn't see the man's face, but she could hear him continue to comment on everything that added to his joy—all buildings and parks they passed. Johnson writes:

> The atmosphere in the bus grew immediately more carefree, as did the woman's heart. The man's enthusiasm was so win-some, the woman found herself smiling. When the bus reached the woman's stop, she worked her way through the crowd to the door. As she did so, she glanced at the "tour guide"—a plump man, wearing dark glasses and carrying a white cane. He was blind.

> As she stepped off the bus, she realized the day's tensions had disappeared. God had sent a blind man to help her see that, though things go wrong sometimes, it's still a beautiful world. [16]

### BOOKS, MUSIC, MOVIES, AND MEDIA

God speaks through media. His voice can be found in books, magazines, albums, movies, radio, and even the Internet. While many believers hear God through Christian media, God can use mainstream or secular sources to speak, too.

My friend Marlene says she was listening to David Wilcox's song, "Eye of the Hurricane," which is about addiction, when God used the lyrics to speak to her. Wilcox writes about a girl who wants to run away but has nowhere to go. She hides in the pouring rain—in the eye of the hurricane. Singing along with the lyrics, Marlene recognized God speaking to her: He was in the center of her storm—ready to cleanse and heal her from the drowning pain.

God can use any form of media—from billboards to book-marks—to speak. God used a movie to speak to James and his wife during a tense moment. James recalls the story: "We were having a fight, a bad one. We were both hurting and sad. We had rented the movie, "The Bear," earlier in the day, and were both so upset we just put the movie in and started watching it.

"About thirty minutes into the movie is a scene where a male bear cub, whose mother died, is following a huge rogue bear. The bear doesn't want the cub to follow. He keeps turning around, growling, and swiping at the cub, but the cub stays just far enough away to keep from harm or attack.

"When they finally make it to the creek, the bear lies down in the muddy shallow (water) and rolls his wounded shoulder into the water and mud trying to cleanse and cover the wound. The cub sneaks up and starts to lick the bear's wounds. At first, the bear tries to ward off the cub but is just too spent to do much about it. Instead, he just lays here and lets the cub minister healing to him. Out of this action, they become pals.

"I got up from my chair, walked over to where my wife, Debbie, was sitting and put my arm cautiously over and around her shoulder. She began to cry and leaned into my chest. I cried, as well. We held each other until we had gathered some composure, then talked about how we felt. We both mentioned that the scene from the movie brought very distinct thoughts to our minds about being wounded and being healed. We found it highly unusual that we had this movie playing, which showed almost exactly what we were going through, at that moment. Yet, there were no words, just beautiful background music by Tchaikovsky.

"To this day, when we see that movie with our kids or anybody, we stop to tell them the deeper meaning of that particular scene—

how much people are like those two bears and the path to joining and restoration of relationships."

Whether it's watching a video, listening to a CD, or thumbing through the pages of a magazine, God can use anything to speak to you.

## PROVISION

One of the tender ways God speaks is through provision. He provided Abraham with a son, Noah with an ark, Isaac with a wife, and the Israelites with manna. Using Elijah, God multiplied a poor widow's flour and oil and even raised her son from the dead to which she responded, "Now I know that you are a man of God, and that the word of the Lord from your mouth is the truth" (1 Kings 17:24).

Jesus was known for feeding the multitudes and using coins from a fish's mouth to pay taxes. Truly, God is God of provision. And while it's easy to recognize the "big ways" in which He provides—house, food, car, job—it's usually those "little ways" that are the most endearing.

A long-time Christian, Karen had experienced God's provision numerous times. The empty nester recently developed a small catering business to help support her family. She bid on a large dinner and was awarded the contract, but the meal required more large white tablecloths than she owned. When she checked with a local renter and dry cleaning company, Karen learned that each cloth would cost twenty-five dollars for the event. She recalculated her bid and discovered the cost of the tablecloths would not only eat away her profit margin, but actually cause her to lose money on the contract.

With only three days left before the event, Karen wasn't sure what she was going to do. While visiting a nearby town, she stopped in a second-hand store. When she walked in the door, she couldn't believe what she saw: a stack of white, folded table cloths—the exact number she needed.

Karen's story reminds us that God is interested in the details of our life. Nothing is impossible for God, and nothing escapes His eye.

## NATURE

It may sound strange to think that God speaks through nature, but Scripture clearly supports this principle. Psalm 19:1 says, "The heavens declare the glory of God; the skies proclaim the work of his hands," and Psalm 97:6 reminds us, "The heavens proclaim His righteousness, and all the peoples see his glory."

God uses nature to communicate and reveal things about Himself. Acts 14:17 says, "Yet he has not left himself without testimony. He has shown kindness by giving you rain from heaven and crops in their seasons; he provides you with plenty of food and fills your hearts with joy."

He uses everything from the weather to small creatures to reveal aspects about Himself. Romans 1:20 says, "For since the creation of the world His invisible attributes, His eternal power and divine nature, have been clearly seen, being understood through what has been made, so that they are without excuse."

A young woman named Eve says God often uses nature to express His unconditional love to her. She remembers sitting on a dock in Wisconsin wrestling with a feeling of having to win God's approval. Winter was approaching and she could hear the leaves clapping together in the crisp autumn wind.

"I realized they were clapping for me ... if I never did anything again for God," Eve recalls. "God still would clap for me, cheer me on and create beautiful sunsets for me to watch and know of His glory."

God can use anything—including the birds of the air and the beasts of fields—to reveal something about Himself and speak eternal truths.

## CRAZY WAYS

God is personal. He knows you intimately. He knows every detail of your life, and sometimes He will speak to you in ways only you will understand. These may seem outlandish to a stranger, but between you and the Father they are recognizable and precious.

My friend Lisa says she (literally) gets pennies from heaven all the time. She will find shiny new pennies in the most bizarre places when she is in the middle of a prayer. Describing these friendly little finds, she says, "I choose to believe they are little hugs from God to say, 'Hey, I'm listening, I hear you.'"

Lisa could choose to believe they are just ordinary pennies on the ground and it's a coincidence that she finds them whenever she's talking with God. Instead, she recognizes them as reminders He is near.

"God's voice is directed to the ear of love, and true love is intent upon hearing even the faintest whisper."

—*Streams in the Desert*[17]

*once you've heard the whisper*

You've been spending time with God. Seeking Him. Talking to Him. You have felt some nudges. You have heard an internal audible voice, received a vision, or felt a strong impression. You are beginning to step out, but you also have some questions. This chapter is designed to tackle some of the most common issues that arise when you are beginning to hear and respond to the Father's voice.

### WAS THAT REALLY GOD

Was that really God? It is one of the most common concerns people have when they hear a whisper. It doesn't always go away with experience. Even long-time Christians revisit this question.

If you're not sure whether or not it was really God speaking to you, here are some questions you need to ask yourself:

(Note: Not all of these questions will apply to every whisper you hear.)

- Does what I heard line up with Scripture?

- Does what I heard line up with circumstance?

- Does what I heard line up with the wise counsel?

- Does what I heard line up with my vision and goals?

- Does what I heard leave me with a sense of peace?

- Is this a thought I would normally think on my own?

- Is what I heard blanketed in love?

Let's go through these questions individually.

*Does what I heard line up with Scripture?*

The Bible serves as your first gauge in determining whether or not a whisper was from God. If you feel led to do something that goes against God's commands, then it isn't from Him. God doesn't tell people to steal, embezzle, gossip, brag, or put others down. He is in the business of loving and redeeming mankind.

While the Bible is a rudder and guide for hearing from God, it may not always speak directly into a circumstance or situation. Should you move to New York or Los Angeles? Should you take a job at one company or the other? Should you marry Melinda or Melissa (assuming both are believers)? That's why there are other questions you need to ask about what you believe God whispered.

*Does what I heard line up with circumstance?*

Sometimes you will think you heard something that doesn't line up with circumstance. You may feel like God is leading you to move somewhere, but your boss doesn't want you to leave and the local church just invited you to become more involved in ministry. Meanwhile, neither a job nor a place to live has opened up where you feel like you're supposed to move.

Clearly, circumstance isn't confirming what you heard. Yes, it may have been God, but He may be whispering something that may not happen for five or even fifteen years. Remember God can open and close doors to move you exactly where He wants you to be. If the doors aren't opening, and you have been faithful in praying and knocking, then trust that the whisper may not be part of His plan, at least for right now.

*Does what I heard line up with the wise counsel?*

Would you build a house without paying a visit to an architect? Would you sail across the Atlantic without spending some time with salty sailors who did it before? Would you buy a used vehicle without talking to an auto mechanic? Probably not.

God places people in your life to provide wisdom and counsel. Maybe it's a parent or pastor. Maybe it's a mentor or boss. Maybe it's a neighbor or friend. If you don't already have strong, godly people who can speak into your life, you need to pursue these types of relationships. Even if the whisper isn't an invitation to do something, it's still a good idea to share what you heard with older, wiser believers who also hear from God and can provide wisdom and advice on your journey.

Godly counsel is invaluable when sorting through issues related to something you have heard from God. Proverbs 15:22 says, "Plans fail for lack of counsel, but with many advisers they succeed."

You may feel God has spoken to you about going to India. A wise counselor will challenge you with a number of practical questions including: When are you going to go? How are you going to get there? What are you going to do when you arrive? Who will be responsible for obtaining your financial support? You may feel the tug at your heartstrings to go, but you still need to address a number of concerns.

You may also find that your counsel is against the trip to India. Without the blessing and support of those who are in godly authority over you, you may want to consider postponing the trip.

They may be seeing or sensing something that you are not. The timing may be off or maybe you are only supposed to go on a short-term trip.

*Does what I heard line up with my vision, goals, and ideas in my life?*

This is a tough one, but sometimes you need to take a step back from what you heard and put it in the overall context of your life. In the church, testimonies abound of people living in little no-name towns being called to be missionaries in other no-name towns on the other side of the world. Some can give compelling stories of how the last thing they ever wanted to do was live in a particular geographic zone or work in a certain profession, and that is exactly what God called them to do.

My friend Shannon, who hates deserts, was sent to Israel as a missionary for several years. It can happen to anyone, even you. But it is not the norm for everyone's life, let alone daily life.

God's plan for most people's life isn't *find out what they hate and then make them do it*. Psalm 37:4-6 promises, "Delight yourself in the LORD and he will give you the desires of your heart. Commit your way to the LORD; trust in him and he will do this: He will make your righteousness shine like the dawn, the justice of your cause like the noonday sun."

Therefore, when you hear a whisper from God, especially one that offers a directive, you need to ask yourself the other questions in this list and put it in the perspective of where God has taken you and where you think He is leading you.

Your church may hold a special week of events that focus on missions, small groups, or giving. You may feel like God is whispering to you through these events. After all, every time you're in church you are being bombarded with the same message. But before you run off to Argentina or sell everything you own, you need to evaluate what you've heard in light of God's plan for your life.

*Does what I heard leave me with a sense of peace?*

In Isaiah 9:6, Jesus is referred to as the "Prince of Peace." Ephesians 2:14 identifies Jesus as our peace. During His short time on earth, Jesus spoke repeatedly of peace and often greeted people with, "Peace be with you," following the customary Jewish greeting, "shalom."

As a believer, you have peace the world cannot comprehend. Peace is a fruit of the Spirit and an attribute of God. Peace is a gift, and it often acts as a guardrail in our lives, warning us when we have stepped outside of God's perfect will or compromised His commands.

Philippians 4:7 promises, "the peace of God, which transcends all understanding will guard *your hearts and minds* in Christ Jesus" (emphasis added). Peace acts as an umpire for your spiritual journey. The level of peace you have in your heart should be considered when evaluating something you heard from God. If you have an uneasy feeling or a sense that something just isn't quite right, then you need to consider seeking the Lord about what you heard before taking any action.

*Is this a thought I would normally think on my own?*

Humans naturally have a self-centered approach to life. While most people will not verbalize it, there is a voice in the back of our minds that screams for self-preservation. Watch out for me. Take care of me. Do what's best for me. I am more important. It centers on protecting and serving self.

God's whispers are different. They tend to focus on what is important to God, not what is important to you. God's whispers are God-oriented. They glorify God. They are pleasing to God. They bring about God's will. They usually aren't focused around the easiest, most pleasurable decisions.

Yes, the whisper may be enjoyable and pleasurable to you, too. It may fulfill a lifelong dream or calling, but usually it is something that will challenge you or benefit others.

*Is what I heard blanketed in love?*

One of the most important gauges to discern whether a whisper is from God is by searching your heart and asking, "Is the whisper blanketed in love?" Love will keep you humble and dependent on God. It will put others' needs above your own. Take what you've heard and reflect on it in the light of 1 Corinthians 13.

If love is protecting your actions and decisions, then you will be restrained from making grievous errors. If your actions and attitudes are bathed in love, it is hard to go wrong.

Love becomes critical if you feel compelled to share the whisper with others. Can you deliver the message in love? Can you deliver it without getting puffed up with pride? Check your motives and hold off on saying anything until you can do so in love.

If you have reflected on these questions and feel you have a green light to step out on what you have heard, go for it. You may stumble. You may fall. You may also see God do something wonderful through your obedience. Either way, the arms of a loving Father will catch you.

## IS IT OKAY TO ASK FOR CONFIRMATION?

Confirmation is a wonderful gift from God. If you feel like you are unsure if you heard from God or are confronting a huge decision and don't want to be wrong, ask God to confirm the whisper you heard. He may speak through a friend, Scripture, circumstance, or any of the other ways discussed in this book.

You do not need to ask for confirmation in every situation. If you feel God leading you to apologize to a friend, deliver a word of encouragement, or give a small gift, you probably don't need God to confirm it to you repeatedly. Beware of using the need for confirmation as a means of avoiding obedience.

## HOW DO I GET RID OF CONFUSION?

As you begin to hear God's whisper, you will undoubtedly begin to question what you heard. Was it God or your mind playing tricks on you? You thought you heard God say "yes" but now you think He's saying "no."

If you are in the thick of a situation, you need to remove yourself from it. You may need to go on a drive or take a long walk. If you have the time, a weekend retreat might be a good idea. Do something to clear your head. Get some exercise. Watch a movie. Grab a bite to eat. Listen to a CD.

Then, revisit the issue with the Lord. Confess the doubt and ask Him to remove any confusion. Ask Him to make it crystal clear to you what He is trying to say. Then, trust He will use whatever it takes to communicate with you.

## WHAT ABOUT WHEN I'M WRONG?

You were convinced God was telling you to do something, but everything falls apart. You were certain you were meant to go somewhere, but every door closes.

If any of these things happen to you, congratulations, you're normal. It's all part of the process. No, it is not fun, and it can be frustrating, disappointing, embarrassing, and confusing, but it is still part of the journey.

Most Christians would like to skip the learning part of hearing God's voice. In essence, they would like to jump from newborn to a five year old so they can walk, talk, and get out of those nasty diapers. Every parent knows children are born completely helpless and dependent. Just as it takes years to go from crawling to jumping the high hurdles, it takes time to recognize, understand and respond to God's voice.

The good news is God knows that, too. He knows you will make mistakes, stumble over your words, and even misunderstand His. It isn't pretty. It isn't enjoyable. And sometimes, like a dirty diaper, it just plain stinks.

You are going to mess up along the way. You are going to misunderstand, misinterpret, and probably even misinform others from time to time. He knows that, and I would even go so far to say He's okay with that. He is not stressed. He is not anxious. He is just excited you are growing and desiring to pursue Him. He promises to work all things for good for those who love Him and are called according to His purpose.

A wealthy woman saw an irresistible bracelet in a store while traveling overseas. She sent her husband an inquiry by cable: "Have found wonderful bracelet. Price $75,000. May I buy it?" Her husband promptly wired back, "No, price too high." But the cable operator forgot to include the comma so the woman received the reply, "No price too high."

She purchased the bracelet. [18]

Do you see the difference one little comma can make?

Sometimes there are commas in the messages God gives us, but in a moment of presumption, exuberance, or impatience, we miss the heartbeat of what God is saying or mistake a burden the Lord may be giving us as a calling.

We have all seen it and experienced it. Someone feels like he's called to missions. Before you know it, he tells everyone he's going to be a missionary to Ecuador for the rest of his life (after all, the person has always wanted to travel and has met three people from Ecuador in the last year, so it must be God). Yet every door for the person to go to Ecuador seems to be closing. He can't raise the funds. He hasn't found the right program. He does not have the support of his church, family or friends. Why?

Because he never took the time to find out exactly what God was saying to him. Yes, God may have whispered missions into his heart, but did He mean short-term or long-term missions? Inner-city or foreign missions? Should he work with a church or national organization? Was he supposed to leave immediately or in twenty years? Was the call to be a missionary or to support missions?

Maybe the person experienced a burden for China rather than a call to China. God was awakening a desire to pray for this nation and support missions, but with time the burden lifted and the desire lessened. Sometimes God will allow a season of prayer for a person, institution, nation, or situation, then it will lift. Burdens are sometimes mistaken for callings. A burden will lessen after time, but a calling will intensify over time.

Whatever the reason for the misunderstanding, we will all experience them. When you're wrong, you have two choices: grow discouraged and become skeptical of other times God tries to speak to you or learn from the experience. The choice is yours.

First Corinthians 13—a chapter focused on love—reminds us, "Now we see but a poor reflection as in a mirror, then we shall see face to face. Now I know in part, then I shall know fully, even as I am fully known."

Let me share some of my dimmer moments. There have been times I thought I had heard the Lord and discovered before the words were even out of my mouth that I was wrong.

In 1997, I thought I was going to Israel. I prayed about Israel. My heart burned for Israel. It seemed like every time I turned on the news, I saw something on Israel (imagine that!). I felt in my heart I had heard the word, "Your feet shall walk in the Holy Land," and I was ready to buy a plane ticket. Somewhere along the line, I thought I heard (or really wanted to hear) "Your feet shall walk in the Holy Land *this year*." Well, needless to say, 1997 came and went and I never set foot in Israel.

Oops. Did God really speak those words? Yes, but probably not the "this year" part. That was either added by my emotions or my own will. I was wrong. Will I go to Israel one day? With a name like Feinberg, I hope so. But it will probably happen on God's timetable, not my own.

I learned several important lessons from that "oops." First, when God speaks something, write it down just as it is when you get it. That way your hopes and imagination can't pollute it later and turn it into something it is not. Second, when you feel like God is giving you something time or date-related, be very careful whom you share it with so you don't end up looking ridiculous if it doesn't come true. Fortunately, that little whisper stayed tucked away in my journal and has only come out for the purpose of this book.

Stories of being wrong abound in my own life. I'd like to share a few so you can feel better about your own. During my junior year of college, I wanted to study abroad in a Spanish speaking country. I prayed and fasted as to where to go. I looked at an atlas, studied up on foreign language programs, and spoke to my university's overseas guidance counselor. I discovered a reasonable program in Salamanca, Spain where I could study Spanish, live with a family and engage in the culture. It sounded great! There was only one problem: my counselor wouldn't approve the program for credit. She would approve other programs, but not the one I wanted to go on.

I went to the chapel one night and began praying. Randomly flipping open the Bible, the page fell to Romans 15, and there I discovered the words that sealed my fate: "I plan to do so when I go to Spain." I couldn't believe my eyes. The very country I was praying about was mentioned in the Bible. If the Apostle Paul was making a trip to Spain, then so was I! God was sending me to Spain to study abroad.

I kept reading just to make sure. In verse 28 it reads, "I will go to Spain and visit you on the way" (emphasis added). If that wasn't double confirmation, then I didn't know what was! My not-so-Christian-attitude was "heck with the guidance counselor"; after all, I had enough credits to graduate without her approval and besides, I had heard from God. (An illustration of why the question *"Does what I heard line up with the wise counsel and authority in my life?"* is so important.)

In a few short months, I was off to the country mentioned twice in Romans 15. Looking back, I think those were probably ninety of the worst days of my life. Everything that could go wrong, doubled itself and did. There were rioters on my flight across the Atlantic, and the plane had to be redirected through England for someone who needed a heart transplant.

I arrived exhausted in Madrid, twenty-some hours later than scheduled, only to discover there are several train stations in the capital city, and only one would take me to Salamanca. Of course, I didn't know enough Spanish to figure out which one.

Within an hour I was lost in downtown Madrid carrying way too much luggage and walking in my socks (because my new boots had cut into the back of my heels until they were bleeding.) Eventually, I found a bus to Salamanca, but the tire blew, which added several hours to an already long journey.

When I finally arrived in my host house, I was exhausted, dirty, and in desperate need of bandages. I had just completed my first day in Spain.

The next eighty-nine were a lot like the first. My host family was horrible. (Yes, bad ones do exist, despite what college and overseas brochures may tell you).

The language school was even worse. I had to change programs and hope for a refund. I was homeless for five days, living in a hotel during the transition. Everything I touched and everywhere I went seemed to fall apart. I was scheduled to be on flights that were canceled, buses that ran out of gas, and trains that broke (I still don't understand how a train breaks). I had a knack for picking the sketchy hostel and arriving at restaurants after they closed. My seventeen-year-old dog died while I was in Spain. A bird even pooped on me.

Yes, I did grow and mature a lot during my time abroad. I discovered God in ways only someone who has hit rock bottom (and fallen further) can know Him. My survival skills were sharpened, and for the rest of my life, I will know how to find food, a hotel, and a bathroom in a Spanish-speaking country.

Now that the experience is years behind me I can safely ask the question, "Was the Lord really telling me to go to Spain?" Maybe. Maybe not. If He was asking me to go, I wasn't asking Him about which program to choose. I picked it for myself and went above my rightfully placed authority and the wisdom of a guidance counselor. There is an umbrella of protection when we are obedient to God and in His perfect will, and I stepped outside into the storm.

Ecclesiastes 8:5-6 says, "Whoever obeys his command will come to no harm, and the wise heart will know the proper time and procedure. For there is a proper time and procedure for every matter." Looking back, I wish I had stumbled upon this verse that fateful day in the chapel rather than the one in Romans. Now whenever

God whispers "go" to me, I am very careful to ask, "Where? How are we going to get there? What are we going to do when we're there? And is there anything You don't want me to do?"

Fortunately, I'm not alone in being wrong. One woman recently told me about a fateful attempt of trying to listen to the Lord through circumstance. She was anxious for a job. After an interview with the first company that called, she told the Lord if this was the job for her then all He needed to do was have the company meet her salary requirements.

The company offered her the full amount, and she accepted. The woman was not in the job two days before she realized things were askew. Within a few weeks she was blamed for thievery within the company and asked to leave. She repented for not fully seeking the Lord about the issue and learned a valuable lesson.

My friend Amanda knew it was time to move. She prayed and in her mind she saw a snowy field and bright orange sun setting in the sky. She thought to herself, God is showing me I am going to move to Alaska. Within three months, she ended up moving to Colorado to be with family rather than Alaska. Looking back on picture she originally saw, she realized she had jumped to the conclusion that if it had snow, it had to be Alaska. As it turned out, God was directing her move to a less snowy state.

Now that you've heard a few glad-that-wasn't-me testimonies, there is a question you must ask yourself: Are you willing to be wrong?

Because you are not going to learn to hear from God without eating humble pie from time to time. Are you willing to forgive God and yourself when it happens? Are you willing to learn from the mistakes?

If you were content with a slower pace, you wouldn't be this far along in this book. The fact is that something inside of you longs to run after the Lord. It yearns to step out in faith, and grow in grace.

So when you are wrong (and you will be), learn from it. Become wiser. Quickly forgive God and yourself. At first, you will probably be a little more hesitant in responding to God's whisper. You will begin questioning more whether something truly is from God. That is normal. It's okay to ask for confirmation. Ask, "What's next, Lord?" and keep going.

Everyone makes mistakes. Just remember the majority of those mistakes come from people who never bothered to seek God or involve Him in the matter. Would you rather be one of those who tried to listen to God and obey with a little stumbling or one who never bothered to listen to Him at all? If you let yourself make mistakes, then you open yourself up to a whole new world of possibility and adventure.

## WHAT ABOUT WHEN I'M WRONG AND IT HURTS?

As a nine year old, Leo Tolstoy believed with all his heart God would help him fly. He was so confident one day he jumped head-first out of a third-story window. In one crashing moment, Tolstoy was introduced to his first big disappointment with God. Many years later, Tolstoy could laugh at his youthful test of faith.[19]

He survived the fall and so did his belief in God, but not everyone walks away from a leap of faith. Sometimes the injury is severe. It can't be laughed off or filed away as one of those (Christian) most embarrassing moments or written off as a bad trip to Spain. The sense of disappointment or disillusionment doesn't fade away. It lingers. It hurts. If left unchecked, it can infect your faith and relationship with God. In some cases, it can be devastating.

If you've been deeply hurt while trying to hear and obey God's voice, you're not alone. In fact, you're among the masses. Learning to hear and recognize God's voice isn't easy. It isn't always fun. Neither for the novice nor for the veteran. Sometimes the pain can be worse in the later years of the Christian journey than in the beginning.

Maybe you heard from God that a certain person was "the one." You knew in your spirit. You had absolute confidence. Everyone around you knew, too. The proposal was rejected, retracted, or never came to pass.

Maybe you were given a vision of what God was going to do in your community, church, or ministry. You can still quote the words He spoke. But when you look around now, everything is a mess. The situation is different all right. Everything has crumbled. The vision is gone. The dream is dead.

Maybe you knew beyond a shadow of a doubt God was going to heal someone, save someone, or repair a relationship. You prayed. You cried out to God. You poured out your tears, your very soul, and He answered you. You held the Scripture, the words, the promise in the palm of your hand. But the health keeps deteriorating. The person refuses to acknowledge God. There has been no reconciliation.

And it hurts. It hurts deeply. You don't know if you can even trust God now. After all, if He didn't come through on that issue, why should you trust He will come through on the next one? If He wasn't good on His word then, why should you believe He will be now? If He disappointed you once, what's to guarantee He won't disappoint you again?

Those are all fair questions. You are right to ask, but it is going to take more than being right to find an answer. It is going to take becoming righteous.

As much as it hurts, as much as you can claim a right to be mad at

God, you are only hurting yourself. I know that is tough to hear. Let me say it again. You are only hurting yourself!

God wants to heal and restore you. He misses you. Even more than you miss Him.

He desires an intimate, life-giving relationship with you, but something is standing in the way: an issue of forgiveness. You need to forgive God. You need to forgive Him for disappointing you and the pain it caused. Then, you need to do something even harder: you need to forgive yourself. Because tucked in a pain that runs so deep is a sense that you somehow failed, too. You didn't do enough. You didn't have enough faith. You were duped. The list of lies goes on.

Those thoughts weren't planted in you by God. Those were from another one, an evil one, the very one who is trying to separate you from God through the disappointment and hurt.

I could offer you a dozen guesses as to why things didn't work out as you thought they would: maybe it really wasn't God speaking, maybe it wasn't His will ... but they are all just guesses and they seem pretty shallow in the depth of your pain. Besides, you have already played the situation through your mind at least a dozen times and know all the possibilities.

Sooner or later, you are going to have to choose to rip the memory tape of the disappointment out of your mind and let God replace it with His love. Despite what may have happened, God is still true. His promises are still valid. His heart is still for you. It's okay to tread slowly. It's okay to be a little gun shy at first. It's only natural. The shell-shocked don't naturally run right back into battle. But you need to get back up and keep moving.

Here is a suggested prayer:

*God,*

*I am sorry I took a step back from You in my heart. _____ was such a disappointment. It hurt then, and it still hurts. I need You to forgive me and heal that hurt. Forgive me for the anger and judgment I've held in my heart against You. Forgive me for believing the lies of the enemy that say You let me down. I humbly admit I don't know every variable and I can't see the big picture. Only You can. I ask that You redeem the outcome of this situation for Your glory.*

*I also choose to forgive myself. I forgive myself for feeling like I didn't have enough faith, that I didn't do enough and that I was foolish to believe I had heard from You. I forgive myself for being wrong.*

*Now, Lord, I ask You to heal the wound. Heal those places where it still hurts. Pour Your love and grace over them. Help me to trust You again. I need You, and I miss You. I want to be close to You. Draw my heart back to Yours.*

*In Jesus' name. Amen.*

Healing takes time. Building trust takes time. God knows that. Depending on the severity of the hurt, two books I would recommend are *Where Is God When It Hurts?* and *Disappointment With God* by Philip Yancey. In these titles, Yancey asks tough questions about human suffering, disillusionment, and disappointment while tenderly reflecting on the faithfulness of God.

As humans, we are limited in our vision and understanding. It is like walking along a Mezzanine floor as an ant. All an ant sees are the ragged edges and broken pieces. It is limited in its scope of understanding.

In the same way, we don't know all that God is doing or the final outcome of events; thus, we must live with a hope and faith that the Mastermind of creation is at work developing something far more beautiful or wondrous than we can comprehend. Joy Dawson beautifully illustrated this in her book, *Forever Ruined For the Ordinary*:

> A friend of mine was suffering greatly and was terminally ill. I diligently sought God to speak to me from His Word if He intended to bring healing. From the clarity of the specific Scriptures given me through several different methods by which God chose to speak, His answer was a resounding "yes."
>
> When the person died, I was shocked and perplexed to say the least. I was desperate for God's explanation. I will never forget His answer, spoken clearly into my spirit. *"I spoke to you and you obeyed by declaring what I had given you. But you don't know what transpired between your friend and Me after I had spoken to you."*
>
> Those words brought great enlightenment and relief. We're never enlightened or surprised by what comes from our own thoughts. But when God speaks there's always an element of wonderment and awe.
>
> This experience helped me never to quickly come to conclusions about the final outcome of my earnest inquiries and sincere steps of obedience and faith to God on behalf of others. [20]

"In the morning, O LORD, you hear my voice; in the morning I lay my requests before you and wait in expectation."

—Psalm 5:3

# growing through whispers and silence

## WHY IS GOD SOMETIMES SILENT?

One of the great benefits of God's silence is it makes you appreciate the times He speaks. God's silence teaches that when the faucet of God's revelation is running, when you can feel His sweet presence and comprehend His sweet words, get all you can get. Drink in all of His revelations and truth you possibly can. Never neglect or ignore His warm invitation to spend time with you. It is precious. And you never know. He may be pouring out on you because a wilderness period is around the next corner. God reserves the right to be silent. He reserves the right to delay answers, leave certain issues unaddressed, and become seemingly quiet.

Why? There are a myriad of reasons.

*You may have asked the wrong question.* You may have asked to know something that God is not ready to reveal or something that could be detrimental to you or someone else if it was revealed.

For example, you meet someone you don't really like. You begin asking God why you aren't getting along with the person and what is wrong with the person. All the while, God wants you to focus on the strengths of the individual.

107

Or you may have an issue in which you jump ahead in your request. You may have placed your house on the market and asked God, "When will you bring a buyer?" But you never bothered to ask Him if you should sell your home in the first place.

*You may be out of God's timing.* There is a story about James Garfield, who before he became President of the United States, served as the principal of Hiram College in Ohio. A father of one of the students asked him whether a course could be simplified so his son could go through more quickly.

Garfield replied, "Certainly, but it all depends on what you want to make of your boy. When God wants to make an oak tree, he takes a hundred years. When he wants to make a squash, he requires only two summers." [21]

Remember, God works on a different timetable. Sometimes the issues that are the most pressing on your heart are not the most pressing on His. He has an order and timing for everything. Ecclesiastes 3:1 reminds us, "There is a time for everything, and a season for every activity under heaven."

Are you willing to wait for the answer?

*You may not be at a place where you can handle the answer.* God may choose not to answer you, because you are not strong enough to handle it.

Corrie ten Boom's father illustrated this truth beautifully when at a young age Corrie asked him a question about sex. Recognizing his daughter's naiveté, his response was laden with wisdom.

> He turned to look at me, as he always did when answering a question, but to my surprise he said nothing. At last he stood up, lifted his traveling case from the rack over our heads, and set it on the floor.

"Will you carry it off the train, Corrie?" he said.

I stood up and tugged at it. It was crammed with the watches and spare parts he had purchased that morning.

"It's too heavy," I said.

"Yes, he said. "And it would be a pretty poor father who would ask his little girl to carry such a load. It's the same way, Corrie, with knowledge. Some knowledge is too heavy for children. When you are older and stronger you can bear it. For now you must trust me to carry it for you."

And I was satisfied. More than satisfied-wonderfully at peace. There were answers to this and all my hard questions-for now I was content to leave them in my father's keeping."[22]

This same theme was explored in the award-winning film "Life Is Beautiful." The movie follows the adventure of a zesty, comical fellow named Guido who falls head over heels (literally) for a young schoolteacher. Their love blossoms into marriage, and they enjoy life with their young son.

Halfway through the film, the family is ripped away from their home and sent to a Nazi concentration camp where Guido does everything he can to hide the horrors of the war from his young son. In this tender, noble story, hiding the boy from the terrible reality of the camp is an act of love, courage, and sacrifice.

This theme is biblical. Jesus once told His disciples, "I have much more to say to you, more than you can now bear" (John 16:12). When Christ was questioned about the act of washing his disciples' feet, he responded, "Now that you know these things, you will be blessed if you do them" (John 13:17). God knows our limitations even better than we do.

*You may be asking about something that is none of your business.* God is all knowing, but humans are not. They were never intended to be. Sometimes you will be asking for information or insight into something that could easily be a distraction or could harden your heart toward a situation or person.

Sometimes God withholds something from you because it can harm you. Remember the tree of the knowledge of good and evil in the Garden of Eden. Genesis 2:17 records God's command, "But you must not eat from the tree of the knowledge of good and evil, for when you eat of it you will surely die."

There is knowledge that God holds back from us for our own good. There may be someone else involved in a situation or group who is supposed to seek the Lord on a particular issue. He is waiting for that person to step up to the plate, not you.

*You may be living with sin or compromise in your life that blocks your ability to hear from God.* If you are living with your boyfriend, God may not be willing to tell you whether or not the person is "the one." If you're cheating on your income taxes, God may not respond to your request for wisdom as to where to invest money.

You may not be in a position to hear an answer. When God is silent, reflect on why He is silent. Do you have sin or compromise in your life? Sin blocks us from God. It's not that God turns His back on us, but that we turn our backs on Him.

Disobedience can be sin. If you have not been obedient to the last thing God asked you to do, why would He entrust you with more? God will often wait for you to be obedient on small things before He will entrust you with larger ones.

Silence is not always a sin issue. You need to reflect on what God may be trying to teach you. Is this a season of growth or testing? Have you been spending enough time with Him to hear from Him?

*Circumstances—both physical and spiritual—may delay God's answer.* Daniel, the famed lion's den survivor, had to wait three weeks before God answered his request because of spiritual warfare.

Daniel 10:12-14 records, "'Do not be afraid, Daniel. Since the first day that you set your mind to gain understanding and to humble yourself before your God, your words were heard, and I have come in response to them. But the prince of the Persian kingdom resisted me twenty-one days. Then Michael, one of the chief princes, came to help me, because I was detained there with the king of Persia. Now I have come to explain to you what will happen to your people in the future, for the vision concerns a time yet to come.'"

Daniel was not the only one who had to wait for God to speak. When Moses went up on Mount Sinai, the glory of the Lord settled on the mountain. According to Exodus 24:16, "For six days the cloud covered the mountain, and on the seventh day the LORD called to Moses from within the cloud."

Scripture records that Jeremiah also had to wait for the word of the Lord (Jeremiah 42:5). Following Christ's ascension, those in the upper room waited forty days before God poured out His spirit upon them and used them to speak in tongues and declare the mighty deeds of God (Acts 2:11).

*God may be withholding an answer because He has something He wants to work out in an individual or group of people's lives that takes time.* There may be things God is trying to teach someone about Himself that requires Him to wait to answer our request because of the people involved.

After being entrusted with great insight into the future, Daniel was told, "Go your way, Daniel, because the words are closed up and sealed until the time of the end" (Daniel 12:9).

*God may be trying to increase your patience, diligence, or faith.* Why is God silent? One of the biggest reasons is to grow our faith. If you have ever seen the picture that accompanies the famous "Footprints" poem, you'll notice there is only one set of footprints in the sand. Those are moments Jesus is carrying you.

But there are also times in the Christian walk when two sets of footprints are spaced further apart. You can walk this part of the journey without being carried. You don't need your hand held. You know the path. You are still in His presence. You are still connected, but at times God will take a step back to grow our faith. Jeremiah 29:12-13 promises, "Then you will call upon me and come and pray to me, and I will listen to you. You will seek me and find me when you seek me with all your heart."

Waiting for God to answer naturally stretches you and demands more patience and perseverance than you may have originally been willing to offer. God is forever loving you and wanting to grow you into the image of His Son. Hebrews 11:6 promises, "Anyone who comes to him must believe that he exists and that he rewards those who earnestly seek him."

In *Disappointment With God*, Philip Yancey observes that we, as humans, have little understanding of what our faith means to God. He writes:

> In some mysterious way, Job's terrible ordeal was "worth" it to God because it went to the core of the entire human experiment. More than Job's faith, the motive behind all creation was at stake. Ever since God took the "risk" of making room for free human beings, faith—true, unbribed, freely offered faith—has had an intrinsic value to God we can barely imagine. There is no better way for us to express love to God than by exercising fidelity to him. [23]

At times, tests of faith can seem like tough love. No matter how difficult life may become, He doesn't want you to give up. He is after your best. He wants to answer your prayer. Keep seeking. Keep knocking, and whatever you do, don't give up too soon.

The bottom line is that while God knows everything, He does not reveal everything even when you ask Him. In Acts 20:22, Paul says, "And now, compelled by the Spirit, I am going to Jerusalem, not knowing what will happen to me there."

In the face of such silence and uncertainty, Paul had grown to a point were His faith did not waiver. He didn't have to know what was going on. He just had to know God. He goes on to write, "I only know that in every city the Holy Spirit warns me that prison and hardships are facing me. However, I consider my life worth nothing to me, if only I may finish the race and complete the task the Lord Jesus has given me—the task of testifying to the gospel of God's grace" (Acts 20:23-24).

Paul wasn't focused on the details of his mission or what was waiting for him during each visit. The Lord had whispered that prison and difficulties were coming. He didn't know the form of the imprisonment, but girded with the limited knowledge, he didn't lose heart or hope. He was focused on God. [24]

## What If I Haven't Heard from God?

You've prayed. You've asked. You've pleaded. You've begged. You've done everything you know to do. You're out of time. The mortgage is due. The car is about to be repossessed. The graduation ceremony is over. The deadlines are upon you. And still, God is silent. What do you do?

It's a fair question. And, there are a small handful of responses. First, never give up. Study and know the promises of God. Are there any promises or whispers He gave you before the recent silence? Cling to those.

Second, don't be surprised if God moves in the final hour. God likes to stretch and strengthen our faith. To do so, He will often wait until the last hour to move on our behalf.

Third, take a step back from the situation and try to remember any times God may have been trying to speak to you. Often, during stressful or trying times, God is speaking. We are simply not listening. Take some time to reflect on the recent past. Has there been any godly counsel, Scripture, or circumstantial leading? Did God speak, and you just missed it?

There are times when God will be silent, and you will be forced to make a decision. Life circumstances dictate something must be done. Maybe your lease is up, and if you don't move out then you'll be fined or even arrested. Maybe your mortgage is due, and the bank won't take "no" for an answer. Maybe the event is tomorrow, and the last flight there leaves in an hour. You are forced to act one way or the other.

If you find yourself pinned in a corner by circumstance, remember God has not left you. He is still with you, and He still desires the best for you. He may not have ordered a skywriting plane for you, but He still wants to lead you.

On a practical level, reflect on your options in light of the questions found at the beginning of chapter five:

- Does the option line up with Scripture?

- Does the option line up with circumstance?

- Does the option line up with the wise counsel?

- Does the option line up with my vision and goals?

- Does the option leave me with a sense of peace?

- Is this an option I would naturally think of on my own?

- Is the option blanketed in love?

When you have an option or answer that aligns with these questions, then step out. It may be one of those stumbling moments, or it may be a tremendous moment of faith and spiritual growth.

## WHY DOES GOD SAY "NO"?

As you seek God's will on various aspects of life, you will eventually hear God say, "No." It may be to an opportunity, relationship, job, or ministry. It may be to any of a thousand different things you ask Him. It may be something you really want. It can be hard to hear "no."

Sometimes God says "no" to let you out of a situation. Elisabeth Elliot observes:

> "Sometimes our prayers for deliverance from conditions which are morally indispensable—that is, conditions which are absolutely necessary to our redemption. God does not grant us those requests. He will not because He loves us with a pure and implacable purpose: that Christ be formed in us." [25]

"No" can be a hard answer to hear, but it isn't the only one. Over the course of a lifetime, God will say many things that aren't easy to hear. He isn't in the ear-tickling business.

Remember the story of the rich ruler's encounter with Christ. The young man's well-polished, well-fed appearance must have stood in stark contrast to Jesus' travel-worn presentation. Yet Jesus didn't soften his reply for the young man: "You still lack one thing. Sell everything you have and give to the poor, and you will have treasure in heaven. Then come, follow me" (Luke 18:22).

Sometimes God will speak hard words to you and then give you a choice: obey or disobey. The temptation is always to do the latter, but the rewards are promised to those who do the former.

Over the last few years, I have asked the Lord for guidance and wisdom on whether to pursue multiple opportunities and repeatedly heard, "No." Only recently have some of the things that He had said "No" to begun to play out and I have been able to see what would have happened if I had disobeyed. In every situation, I thank God for saving me from the heartache, pain, and disappointment that would have followed.

"No" can be one of God's kindest replies. He knows what is best for us, and when we are reaching for bronze, He reminds us gold is available if we will just wait on Him.

## How Do I Avoid Looking Like a Flake?

If you aren't already asking yourself this question, you should be. You have heard the phrases, "God told me..." or "God is going to..." And, it does not happen. The claim doesn't pan out. You are left with one of two conclusions: either the person was off base or God didn't come through. And it's probably not the latter.

The result is a long list of abuses and unnecessary pain in the body of Christ. Rather than add to the list of abuses of hearing from God, I encourage you to follow the practice of Mary. God whispered to Jesus' mother many times about her special Son. Scripture records that Mary was overshadowed by the Most High. The angel Gabriel made a personal visit. She witnessed the miracles surrounding her relative Elizabeth when she became pregnant and gave birth to John the Baptist. When her Son was finally born, wise men delivered gifts and strangers visited their humble stable. In the face of so much God activity and numerous whispers, Luke 2:19 reveals Mary did something very wise: she "treasured up all these things and pondered them in her heart."

116

She knew that God whispers are really treasures, and they need to be treated as such. Whenever God whispers something to you, hold it in high regard. Keep it near your heart. Let it roll over in your mind and spirit. Recognize the words He is speaking to you are sacred and often meant just for you.

Never forget that God has secrets. He is an all-knowing, all-encompassing God, and He has things He simply chooses not to share with everyone. First Corinthians 2:7 says, "No, we speak of God's secret wisdom, a wisdom that has been hidden and that God destined for our glory before time began." Daniel 2:22 describes God as one who "reveals deep and hidden things; he knows what lies in darkness, and light dwells with him."

Christ revealed some of God's secrets and fulfilled what was spoken through the prophets as one who "will open my mouth in parables" and "utter things hidden since the creation of the world" (Matthew 13:35). Paul reflected on this hidden wisdom as "God's secret wisdom, a wisdom that has been hidden and that God destined for our glory before time began" (1 Corinthians 2:7).

God is not a motor mouth; many times it is important for you to keep things between yourselves.

## WHEN CAN I SHARE THE WHISPER WITH SOMEONE ELSE?

There are times, however, when it's appropriate to share. For example, when a whisper involves a large group of people or something God is going to do within a community. But before you share, I would encourage you to ask yourself the following as safeguards:

- Am I open to correction if I'm wrong?

- Is there anyone I need to get permission from to share this whisper? (pastor, leader etc.)

- Am I willing to be silent if the authority over me asks me to not deliver the message?

- Could anyone be hurt by sharing this whisper?

- Will I be made to look like a fool if it isn't fulfilled?

- Will another person be embarrassed if this isn't fulfilled?

- Will God be embarrassed if this isn't fulfilled?

- Will my word be less credible if this isn't fulfilled?

If you feel led to share what you've heard from God, then be wise with your words. At all costs, avoid using phrases such as, "Thus saith the Lord," "God told me," and "God said." To most people, these phrases suggest you heard audibly and with 100 percent precision. Which, if you didn't, will be misleading. It will also conjure up most people's memories of encounters with false prophets and overly zealous church members.

The "Thus-saith-the-Lord" approach also makes people not want to confront or correct you. When you use that particular phrase, most people are uncomfortable with challenging the message, even though it may really need to be questioned. Some believers have a difficult time with prophetic words and taking this approach may make it harder for them to receive the message.

Temper your words instead. Use phrases such as, "I was praying, and I think God was showing me ...," "I feel like God was impressing on my heart ..." or "I can't explain it, but I just have this sense that ..."

On the surface, using qualifiers may seem to weaken the message, but if God is in the message, then it will grip people's hearts no matter what phrase you use. Using such phrases will also give God more time to work.

There are times when others can learn from the whispers you've heard—whether it's a word of correction or revelation. Be sensitive to the Holy Spirit's leading as to when to share those words.

If you're an eager beaver to tell everyone every single thing you hear from the Lord, then it's probably time to reflect on some of the Old Testament passages that mention what happens to false or disobedient prophets. It will give you a healthy fear of God.

"In our desire after God let us keep always in mind God also has desire, and His desire is toward ... those sons of men who will make the once-for-all decision to exalt Him over all."

—A.W. Tozer[26]

# the invitation of the voice

When a friend calls you, how do you know it's your friend and not just a prank caller? How do you know it's your friend and not your mother, father, brother, boss, or neighbor?

You know because you know your friend. By spending time with your friend, you know the average speed of the person's words. You know the inflections. You recognize the tones. You know the voice. That is the way it should be with God.

You know Him—His character, His nature, His word, His interests, His pleasures and displeasure, His joys and hurts—so well that you recognize Him and His involvement in your life.

If you don't recognize someone's voice, it may mean you haven't been listening. If you don't recognize someone's voice, it may mean you haven't been spending enough time with the person. If you don't recognize someone's voice, it may mean you need to get to know the person better.

God is inviting you to know more than just His voice; He is inviting you to know Him. It's an awesome opportunity. Elijah is a man who accepted the invitation. Even at his lowest moments, he could still discern the word of the Lord. First Kings 19 describes the famed prophet tucked away in a cave.

"What are you doing here?" the Lord asked.

Exhausted and disgruntled, Elijah explained, "I have been zealous for you, but everyone else has rejected your promises, broken down your altars and killed the other prophets. Now I'm the only one left, and they're going to kill me, too."

Elijah was ready to call it quits, but the Lord didn't immediately answer the prophet's concerns. Instead, He asked the prophet to do something a little odd: go out and stand on the mountain and wait. God was going to pass by.

Elijah obeyed. Waiting in one of the mountain's many caves, Elijah could hear the breeze beginning to pick up. Before he could tuck himself any further in the cave, a thunderous wind hit the mountainside, shattering rocks in all its fierceness. But the Lord was not in the wind. A few moments later Elijah could feel the ground tremble; he began to lose his footing. A violent earthquake shook everything that seemed unshakable. But the Lord was not in the earthquake. Then a sudden blaze of heat, an actual fire, came down from heaven. But the Lord was not in the fire. Elijah's heart was filled with fear. What would be next? A lightning bolt? A flood? A volcanic outburst?

Elijah waited. In the still silence, Elijah could hear a gentle whisper. He knew it was the Lord. He got up and "pulled his cloak over his face and went out and stood at the mouth of the cave" (1 Kings 19:13).

The quiet voice asked Elijah the same question it had before: "What are you doing here?" To which Elijah gave the same reply. Then, the Lord answered Him with specific instructions and encouraged him that he was not the only one—there were 7,000 others who had not bowed their knee to Baal.

God pulled the unexpected on Elijah. Rather than give an answer,

God gave Himself. Rather than manifest Himself in all His brilliant glory and splendid power, He chose to use a whisper.

God doesn't always whisper. Sometimes He shouts and creates quite a clamor. When God visited Moses and the multitudes at Mt. Sinai, he didn't use His "inside voice."

Exodus 19:16-20 describes: "On the morning of the third day there was thunder and lightning, with a thick cloud over the mountain, and a very loud trumpet blast. Everyone in the camp trembled. Then Moses led the people out of the camp to meet with God, and they stood at the foot of the mountain. Mount Sinai was covered with smoke, because the LORD descended on it in fire. The smoke billowed up from it like smoke from a furnace, the whole mountain trembled violently, and the sound of the trumpet grew louder and louder. Then Moses spoke and the voice of God answered him."

Both Moses and Elijah knew God well enough to recognize Him in the midst of a cacophony of action and noise. They knew God well enough to recognize Him, not just the signs of Him.

This book could have been titled *God Thunders* or *God Quakes* and still have been taken from the Scripture. It is titled *God Whispers* because the real focus isn't as much about how God speaks as it is about the posture of our relationship with Him.

To hear someone's whisper, you need to be near him or her. Whispering doesn't work very well if the person you are speaking to is on the other side of the room. God isn't content with a long-distance relationship; He wants an intimate one. The posture of this type of relationship is found in John 13:23: "There was reclining on Jesus' breast one of His disciples, whom Jesus loved" (NAS).

It's an intimate portrait. John, believed to be the one described in this verse, is nestled against the Messiah's chest—an expression of reliance and vulnerability. It feels warm and safe. As John turns his head, he can hear the steady heartbeat of his teacher, savior, and friend. It probably wasn't the first time this disciple—who had built a special relationship with Jesus—felt the Master's warm embrace, but unlike previous times, this was a precarious moment in history: the evening of Jesus' betrayal.

Jesus announces that the betrayer is at the table. The disciples perform a quick audit of each other and their own hearts. Breaking the silence, the rock of the group, Simon Peter, looks around the table and gestures to John, "Tell us who it is of whom He is speaking" (v. 24, NAS). The request seems uncharacteristic for the outspoken disciple. Simon Peter is anything but a shy guy. He never had a problem speaking up before, but now his tongue is tied. It's a simple question, but Simon Peter defers it to the one closest to Christ.

"Lord, who is it?" the disciple asks. Jesus exposes Judas.

On the eve of the announcement of Jesus' betrayal, anyone could have been leaning against Jesus' breast. During the previous three years of ministry, multitudes followed Him. In a commissioning, He sent out seventy-two to do the work of the Father. He called twelve to be His disciples. Three were permitted to visit the Mount where Jesus was transfigured. But on that fateful night, only one was leaning against His breast.

What are you leaning against? I believe that the position of being poised against Jesus' breast is available to every believer.

British preacher Alexander Maclaren once observed, "We are able to have as much of God as we want. Christ puts the key to His treasure chest in our hands and invites us to take all we desire. If someone is allowed into a bank vault, told to help himself to the money, and leaves without one cent, whose fault is it if he remains poor? And whose fault is it that Christians usually have some meager portions of the free riches of God?" [27]

How much of God do you really want?

## THE URGENCY OF THE INVITATION

Jesus says, "Here I am! I stand at the door and knock. If anyone hears my voice and opens the door, I will come in and eat with him, and he with me" (Revelation 3:20). This verse isn't just an invitation to become a believer; it's an invitation to live as one.

Notice that Jesus comes to the door empty-handed. He doesn't say, "Open the door and I'll give you a signed and sealed salvation card or a basket full of blessings." In fact, He doesn't bring anything: just Himself. And a small promise to dine together.

Jesus isn't knocking to see what He can give or what He can get. He is knocking because He wants to share a relationship. That is His focus.

I believe we live in an hour when Jesus' knock is becoming more urgent. Like John on the night of Jesus' betrayal, we are living in precarious times. It's not just nice, but necessary to have a deep, intimate relationship with God.

Doug Metzger, author of *Liberty Through The Cross*, describes a vision he had of how the Church was formed in America. God gave him the image of rain falling upon a range of mountains. As the rain fell, it drained down the path of least resistance, ending at the base of the mountains in a desert. The water collected at the desert floor until it developed into a vast lake. Standing at the shore, you could see nothing but water in every direction. As soon as the sun came up, the lake dried up because it didn't have any depth.

The Lord spoke to Metzger's heart and said, "*This is the Church in*

*America. It was formed through following the path of least resistance. It is vast. It is huge. But as soon as there is some heat, it will dry up. Except for a few pools that have a little bit of depth."*[28]

How do you have depth? How do you anchor yourself in the knowledge of God so that no matter what happens—whether the winds of prosperity or adversity blow over—you remain in Him? The answer is simple: by knowing Him.

Living out that answer will cost you everything. It will require sacrifice, dying to self, and choosing the things of God over the things of this world.

Wherever you are and whatever you are doing, God wants to take you one step further. If you have a strong relationship with Him, He wants to make it stronger. If you have discovered deep things of God, He wants to take you deeper. If you are living a holy life, He wants to make you more holy.

Whenever God thinks of you, He has your best in mind. He has plans to take you further, deeper, and higher than you have ever dreamed, but it is hard to get there if you are not listening. It's going to be tough to go anywhere significant if you are more plugged into the television than you are to God. It's going to be hard to complete the journey if you're spending more of your time at the mall than listening to His message. It's going to be nearly impossible to receive His best if you're working more than you're willing to obey.

How do you deepen your relationship with God? By seeking God and looking for ways to spend more time with Him. Who are the people in your life that you have the deepest relationships with? Those who you have spent the most time with. If you reflect on those relationships, you will recognize there were many opportunities when you had to pick up the phone, write the letter, or send the email to contact them.

Though the devices are different, building a relationship with God is the same. You have to turn off the television, open your Bible, get down on your knees, and seek Him. You can't continue your life the way it is and still grow to your full potential in God.

Insanity has been defined as "doing the same things and expecting different results." Spiritual insanity is living the same life and expecting different results. If you want more of God, then you are going to have to change your schedule and priorities.

In a prayer for mercy and help, the prophet Isaiah laments that there is no one "who arouses himself to take hold of Thee" (Isaiah 64:7, NAS).

Where do you begin? Try doubling the amount of time you spend with Him each day. Try doubling the amount of time you spend reading the Bible. Try doubling any of your spiritual disciplines as well as exploring different ones. Memorize Scripture. Journal. Evangelize. Find a mentor. Mentor others.

How do you get to know God? The same way you would a friend. Think about it. You would call the person. You would invite the person over to share a meal. You would listen. You would share. You would look for ways to serve. You would find out what the person likes or dislikes. You would take trips together. Look for every opportunity to know God.

Consider your daily schedule. What does it include? A workout at the gym? A trip to the post office? A lunch hour? A commute? Look for ways to include God in your activities. Invite Him to accompany you by talking to Him. Look for moments—even if it's only ten or twenty seconds—to steal away with Him. It will require effort, but it is possible to reshape your inner life so it is focused around Him. As you seek Him, you will find yourself abiding in Him.

Jesus' invitation isn't only to know God but to abide in Him. John 15:4-5 says, "Remain in Me, and I will remain in you. No branch can bear fruit by itself, it must remain in the vine. Neither can you bear fruit unless you remain in me. I am the vine; you are the branches. If a man remains in me and I in him, he will bear much fruit; apart from me you can do nothing."

Jesus' command to abide in Him is actually an invitation to live in the presence of God. It is a place of rest and quiet confidence where God is in charge.

In *Liberty Through The Cross*, Doug Metzer writes, "What is abiding? It literally means 'to continue to be present' or 'to be held or kept continually.' It is a posture of being poised towards God. It is being able to discern God's voice and knowing how to act upon what He speaks to your heart. It is knowing God as He is. Abiding is embracing and living in the access to the Father that Jesus purchased with His blood." [29]

Abiding implies dependence. Metzer colorfully explains that abiding is "standing in God, though all hell comes against us, knowing He is the author and finisher of our faith. Abiding is not doing. Abiding is being." [30]

When Jesus spent time with His disciples, He provided a portrait of abiding. He ate meals with them. He traveled with them. He talked, laughed, and shared with them. Before Jesus expressed the importance of abiding in John 15, He lived it with them. John 14:25 says, "These things I have spoken to you, while abiding with you" (NAS).

A Bible professor once told his class that in the morning during his prayer time he had asked the Holy Spirit to stay with Him that day. He asked the Holy Spirit not to leave Him. He heard the Holy Spirit respond, *"You don't leave me."*

That should become the goal of our lives—to walk with Him daily. Though I still stumble, I have discovered that listening and obeying God is one of the richest and most rewarding aspects of life. Like the Israelites in the desert, I have found God's whispers to be like manna—something I need every day.

The Israelites didn't wake up in their tents with full stomachs every morning, they had to go out and gather the precious, life-giving bread. In the same way, I need to gather God's Word and wisdom for my life every day.

When I don't take time to be with God and hear Him, I start to lose my way. I lose sight of His promises, what He intends for me, and what He thinks of me. I begin focusing on the world and listening to its messages instead. It usually isn't long before I find myself starving spiritually for God. Now that I've tasted of His treasures and His kingdom, the world just doesn't satisfy. I want more of Him.

Why? Because He is beyond amazing. Some of the whispers I've heard over the years have transformed the way I live and interact with the world. I remember several years ago sitting in the front row of small church in a suburb of Tegucigalpa, Honduras. Even after developing survival-like Spanish skills during my stint in Spain, I still couldn't understand the lyrics during worship, but I could sense God's presence.

I stood with my eyes closed worshipping God when I began to see a picture of the wonder of God's creation. I could see the ocean, all different types of vegetation and various landforms. In my heart, I had a sense of the joy God felt when He formed the world. In the final scene of this ongoing visual movie that played in my mind's eye, I saw a picture of Christ with his hands extended standing beneath a waterfall. Animals of all different species, birds, deer, monkeys—everything imaginable—emerged from where His hands were extended and filled the earth.

By the time the vision was complete, I was literally shaking because of the vivid images and power of God's presence. For the days following the vision, I had the most unusual experience. I could actually hear creation glorifying God. At times, it was so loud it was nearly deafening. We would drive along the mountainous roads outside Honduras' capital city, and I could hear every piece of creation cry out, "Glory, Glory, Glory." The trees, the mountains, the cows in the pasture, the clouds in the sky were all crying "glory" to God. Things you would never consider—mud puddles, gravel, brown grass—were crying "glory" to God with equal fervency. Through this experience, I realized one of my greatest purposes in life is to join with creation crying "Glory, Glory, Glory" with my mouth, heart, strength, and life.

After three days, the crying of creation within my spirit slowly abated. In the following weeks, I began reading Scriptures with a new understanding. Luke 19:37-40 says:

> When he came near the place where the road goes down the Mount of Olives, the whole crowd of disciples began joyfully to praise God in loud voices for all the miracles they had seen: "Blessed is the king who comes in the name of the Lord!"
>
> "Peace in heaven and glory in the highest!"
>
> Some of the Pharisees in the crowd said to Jesus, "Teacher, rebuke your disciples!"
>
> "I tell you," he replied, "if they keep quiet, the stones will cry out."

After my experience, I realized Jesus wasn't kidding around. The very rocks of the earth would cry out. In fact, I believe they already are. We just can't always hear them.

I also began reading Romans 8, where Paul speaks of creation "groaning," in a new light and depth of understanding. I finally grasped how the four living creatures John describes in the worship around the throne never cease saying, "Holy, holy, holy is the Lord God Almighty, who was, and is, and is to come" (Revelation 4:8). Such few words for all of eternity are more than enough.

The experience also gave me a deeper revelation of Christ's presence and involvement in creation. The Genesis account is chocked full of so many "God said" and "God made" that it's easy to forget Christ was there, too. In Genesis 1:26, it says, "Then God said, 'Let *us* make man in our image, in *our* likeness'" (emphasis added). The same Christ who walked the earth is the same one who was part of forming the earth and filling it with life.

Though the vision is now years behind me, I'll be out hiking from time to time and hear the quiet whisper of "Glory, Glory, Glory" within my spirit; it's a reminder of God's presence, glory, and dominion throughout the earth.

This type of experience moves me from having knowledge of God in my head to having knowledge of God in my heart. I know more about Him. I see His presence in new ways. I am not alone. I live in a generation that is hungry for God.

This generation is spiritually starved for His presence. We want to know Him, and we want to be around people who know Him.

If we are going to be God's people and part of His kingdom, then we have to know Him. We must have more than information about God to offer, we must have God dwelling within us. When people come to us seeking answers, we must offer them more than pat answers or religious clichés.

More information is available to this generation than any other in the history of the world. Developments in numerous fields—scientific, historical, philosophical, technological—result in count-less articles which include new facts, statistics, quotes, and trends. Yet when most people ask questions about God, they aren't looking for information. If they did, they could go online or visit a library. They want to talk to someone who knows Him.

If you wanted to know about the President, would you rather speak with a person who read a book about the President or a person who had dinner with the President last week at the White House?[31] Which would you choose? Most people would choose to hear the details of the dinner engagement. After all, you could hear about the book some other time or pick up your own copy. But dinner with the President! This person could share intimate details like what the President likes to eat, what the White House dining room looks like, what the President was wearing, what's it like to be with him, and maybe tell a funny story or two.

Most people will choose to spend time with someone who has intimate knowledge of God over someone who just knows some information about Him. This generation wants to be around people who know God and have heard from Him. They want to be around people who don't just know God's principles but who have paid a price, walked them out, and have born fruit through their faithfulness.

How can we become the people of God that we are intended to be? By learning to hear and obey God's voice.

May God whispers become a part of your everyday.

# SOURCES

[1] Tozer, A.W. *The Pursuit of God* (Camp Hill: Christian Publications, 1982), p. 50. Used with permission of publisher.

[2] McDonough, John. "Jokes of the Century," *The Wall Street Journal*, November 6, 1997, p. A20.

[3] Tozer, A.W. *The Pursuit of God* (Camp Hill: Christian Publications, 1982), p. 54. Used with permission of publisher.

[4] Cymbala, Jim. *Fresh Wind, Fresh Fire* (Grand Rapids: Zondervan, 1997), p. 141-143. Taken from *Fresh Wind, Fresh Fire.* Copyright 1997 by Zondervan Publishing House. Used by Permission of Zondervan.

[5] From *Nelson's Illustrated Bible Dictionary*, "Animals" Copyright (c)1986, Thomas Nelson Publishers.

[6] Ten Boom, Corrie. *The Hiding Place.* (Grand Rapids: Chosen, 1996), p. 33. Used with permission.

[7] Adapted from Gray, Alice. *Stories for the Heart.* (Sisters: Multnomah, 2001), p. 250-251.

[8] Ten Boom, Corrie. *The Hiding Place.* (Grand Rapids: Chosen, 1996), p. 63. Used with permission.

[9] Hill, S.J. *Enjoying God.* (Lake Mary: Relevant, 2001), p. 143. Used with permission of publisher.

[10] Hill, S.J. *Enjoying God.* (Lake Mary: Relevant, 2001), p. 143. Used with permission.

[11] Elliot, Elisabeth. *A Lamp For My Feet.* (Ann Arbor: Vine Books, 1985), p. 50. From *A Lamp For My Feet* by Elisabeth Elliot. 1985 by Elisabeth Elliot. Published by Servant Publications, P.O. Box 8617, Ann Arbor, Michigan, 48107. Used with permission.

[12] Blackaby, Henry and King, Claude. *Experiencing God.* (Nashville: Broadman & Holman, 1994), p. 38.

[13] Parish, Fawn. *It's All About You, Jesus.* (Nashville: Thomas Nelson, 2001), p. 178-179. Used with permission of author.

[14] Virkler, Mark. *You Can Hear God's Voice* (CWG Ministries) brochure from www.cwgministries.org or (800)466-6961. Used with permission.

[15] Peace, Richard. *Spiritual Journaling: Recording Your Journey Toward God.* (Colorado Springs: NavPress, 1995), p. 9. Taken from *Spiritual Journaling: Recording Your Journey Toward God.* Richard Peace. 1996. Used by permission of NavPress (www.navpress.com). All rights reserved.

[16] Individual story by Barbara Johnson. *Stories of Hope for a Healthy Soul.* (Grand Rapids:

Zondervan Gifts, 1999), p. 17. Taken from *Stories of Hope for a Healthy Soul.* Copyright 1999 by Zondervan Publishing House. Used by permission of Zondervan.

[17] Cowman, L.B. *Streams in the Desert.* (Grand Rapids: Zondervan, 1997), p. 373.

[18] Morgan, Robert J. *Nelson's Complete Book of Stories, Illustrations & Quotes.* (Nashville: Thomas Nelson, 2000), p. 219.

[19] Yancey, Philip. *Disappointment With God.* (Grand Rapids: Zondervan, 1988), p. 77. Taken from *Disappointment With God.* Copyright 1988 by Zondervan Publishing House. Used by permission of Zondervan.

[20] Dawson, Joy. *Forever Ruined For the Ordinary: The Adventure of Hearing and Obeying God's Voice.* (Nashville: Thomas Nelson, 2001), p. 128-9. Used with permission of author.

[21] Morgan, Robert J. *Nelson's Complete Book of Stories, Illustrations & Quotes.* (Nashville: Thomas Nelson, 2000), p. 601.

[22] Ten Boom, Corrie. *The Hiding Place.* (Grand Rapids: Chosen, 1996), p. 30-31. Used with permission.

[23] Yancey, Philip. *Disappointment With God.* (Grand Rapids: Zondervan, 1988), p. 209. Taken from *Disappointment With God.* Copyright 1988 by Zondervan Publishing House. Used by permission of Zondervan.

[24] "Many Reasons Why God Delays Answers" from Joy Dawson's *Forever Ruined For the Ordinary* (Nashville: Thomas Nelson), pp. 90-110 was helpful in writing this section on God's silence.

[25] Elliot, Elisabeth. *A Lamp For My Feet.* (Ann Arbor: Vine Books, 1985), p. 131. From *A Lamp For My Feet* by Elisabeth Elliot. 1985 by Elisabeth Elliot. Published by Servant Publications, P.O. Box 8617, Ann Arbor, Michigan, 48107. Used with permission.

[26] Tozer, A.W. *The Pursuit of God* (Camp Hill: Christian Publications, 1982), p. 100-101. Used with permission of publisher.

[27] Cowman, L.B. *Streams in the Desert.* (Grand Rapids: Zondervan, 1997), p. 83. Taken from *Streams in the Desert.* Copyright 1997 by Zondervan Publishing House. Used by permission of Zondervan.

[28] Metzger, Doug. *Liberty Through The Cross.* (Self-published, 2000), p. 96-97.

[29] Metzger, Doug. *Liberty Through The Cross.* (Self-published, 2000), p. 70.

[30] Metzger, Doug. *Liberty Through The Cross.* (Self-published, 2000), p. 71-72.

[31] I've never had dinner with the President, but I certainly wouldn't turn down an invitation.

# GO DEEPER.
## Check out other great titles from Relevant.

### I AM RELEVANT:
*A GENERATION IMPACTING THEIR WORLD THROUGH FAITH*

Every day, hundreds of forward-thinking, spiritually hungry twentysomethings impact their world by being relevant to their culture. I AM RELEVANT profiles people ages 18-34 who are doing something deep, something tangible, something passionate to impact our world.

### ENJOYING GOD:
*EXPERIENCING INTIMACY WITH THE HEAVENLY FATHER*

*Enjoying God* challenges and encourages believers of all ages to pursue a passionate and intimate relationship with God. It exposes how misunderstandings of the Father can damage and jeopardize your faith, and uncovers a biblical understanding of God as Father.

### ENTER THE WORSHIP CIRCLE

Through a series of seven voices, the *Enter The Worship Circle* book weaves storytelling and personal reflection into a journey that fuses the modern world with the mystical. Each voice speaks into the adventure of worship, God, eternity and human experience from a different angle.

## [RELEVANTBOOKS]
### WWW.RELEVANT-BOOKS.COM